'*Psychoanalysis in Play* is a significant contribution to contemporary psychoanalysis, offering a nuanced exploration of the interplay between fantasy, isolation, and concealment and the subtle ways patients construct protective illusions, sustain unconscious erotic ties, and shield forbidden attachments through creative disguises. Cooper skillfully integrates classical psychoanalytic foundations with the ideas of Winnicott, Bion, Britton, and Steiner, mapping a continuum from neurotic defenses to more entrenched schizoid dynamics. Central to this process is the concept of "playing," which the author masterfully presents through vivid clinical examples as both a therapeutic tool and a lens for understanding how patients reveal, explore, and transform unconscious patterns. Equally compelling is the book's exploration of temporality, the delicate construction of trust, and the analytic setting's capacity to foster creativity and psychic growth, offering fresh perspectives on the therapeutic process. I strongly recommend it to analysts, therapists, and students interested in the treatment of psychological suffering, as well as to scholars in the human sciences for its profound reflections on the fabric of the human psyche.'

Giuseppe Civitarese, *author of* Psychoanalytic Field Theory: A Contemporary Introduction, *(2023)*

'To read the work of Steven Cooper is to be invited into a world of thoughtfulness. In *Psychoanalysis in Play* he displays his adeptness with psychoanalytic theory utilizing the multiple vertices that accompany an active analytic interrogation of transference-countertransference. His reader is expertly guided through areas of play and paradox, fixation and fantasy, as he uses both classical and contemporary theorists to think about his patient's inner object worlds, carefully finding his way with each individual patient in each individual moment, seeking to determine who he may be for his patient or what he might be holding of theirs, and what his countertransference may be offering to bring into his awareness. Cooper's description of his analytic work with his patients demonstrates his virtuoso abilities to play what Whitman called "the instruments inside us."'

Bruce Reis, PhD, FIPA, BCPsa, *North American Regional Editor,* International Journal of Psychoanalysis

Psychoanalysis in Play

In this book, Steven H. Cooper expands on his thinking of psychoanalysis as a form of play and the implications of this for theory and clinical practice.

The most important activities of the analyst as a usable object for the patient have to do with finding the patient's creative elements of self. Cooper illuminates this process of finding within both patient and analyst. He illuminates how play processes occur in relation to such concepts as defense, temporality, and neutrality within the analytic situation. Along the way, he theorizes a complex but usable clinical relationship between becoming and knowing in psychoanalytic work.

With rich clinical vignettes and a fresh take on the nature and practice of psychoanalysis, this book is key reading for all psychoanalysts and psychoanalytic psychotherapists.

Steven H. Cooper is a Training and Supervising Analyst at the Boston Psychoanalytic Society and Institute, and the Columbia Center for Psychoanalytic Training and Research, where he is also Clinical Professor of Psychiatry. He has authored five books and coedited two others. He is in practice in New York City.

Psychoanalysis in Play

Expanding Psychoanalytic Concepts from a Play Perspective

Steven H. Cooper

Routledge
Taylor & Francis Group
LONDON AND NEW YORK

Designed cover image: © Hans Guggenheim

First published 2026
by Routledge
4 Park Square, Milton Park, Abingdon, Oxon OX14 4RN

and by Routledge
605 Third Avenue, New York, NY 10158

Routledge is an imprint of the Taylor & Francis Group, an informa business

British Library Cataloguing-in-Publication Data
A catalogue record for this book is available from the British Library

ISBN: 978-1-032-94295-7 (hbk)
ISBN: 978-1-032-94194-3 (pbk)
ISBN: 978-1-003-56998-5 (ebk)

DOI: 10.4324/9781003569985

Typeset in Optima
by Deanta Global Publishing Services, Chennai, India

For Gwen, Ben, and Danny with Love

Contents

Acknowledgments

First, thank you to my patients who teach me continuously about what it is to be a psychoanalyst. I am grateful to be able to do the work that has been so meaningful to me and to learn how to do it better over the years.

Thank you to my wife Gwen, who is always my partner in play. I appreciate many friends with whom I speak about psychoanalysis, especially Ken Corbett, Phil Blumberg, Jim Frosch, Mark O'Connell, Richard Zimmer, Elizabeth Harvey, Elliot Schildkrout, Bernard Edelstein, Jonathan Kolb, and Phillip Freeman.

Thank you to my old friend Hans Guggenheim who offered the drawing on the front cover of this book.

I feel so lucky to have been close to two dear friends who are now gone. Tony Kris was first a mentor, then a collaborator in writing and teaching, and for 30 years a very close friend. Lucy Lafarge was a great friend and intellectual companion for many years. I miss them both.

Introduction

My intention in writing this book and some of the papers that are included was to further elaborate how I view playing in the analysis of adults. In an earlier volume, *Playing and Becoming in Psychoanalysis* (Cooper, 2023a), I developed a contemporary view of playing, one that examined play in relation to the analytic setting, unsymbolized experience, mourning, and ethical dimensions of the analytic process.

In this volume, I examine some additional psychoanalytic concepts in relation to play, such as defense, temporality, and neutrality. I will also examine the types of playing that occur in the analytic process related to the Oedipus complex. Finally, I explore the analyst's "aesthetic matrix" (Palmer, 2023) as an essential part of playing in the analytic process.

In considering a number of core clinical concepts from the perspective of play, I wanted to explore how the underlying logic of psychoanalysis is play (e.g., Parsons, 1999; Cooper, 2018; Cooper , 2023a,b). For example, I tried to theorize how the concept of neutrality applies to play by developing a theory of holding paradox in the context of play. I realized that, in some ways, I viewed the revolutionary work of Winnicott and Bion as occurring in a context in which they each felt that clinical analysis at the time was too skewed toward interpretations or elaborations of unconscious fantasy and defense. In some sense, they were each arguing that such an approach was limited in expanding a patient's sense of aliveness. The attempt to find aliveness and creativity became a central focal point for therapeutic action and ways of thinking about the analyst's neutrality. So I explored how their focus might relate to the concept of neutrality.

In Chapter 1, I address how we can conceptualize defense analysis and the emergence of defenses in analysis from a play perspective. When Winnicott (1959) developed a new theory of defense in his paper on true self and false self, he suggested that defenses are not only organized against impulses that cause anxiety and disruption. He was suggesting that in some families, children develop defenses against objects since the objects themselves not only fail to comfort the child but also become sources of anxiety in their own right, either through specious reality testing or a narcissistic vulnerability of their own.

DOI: 10.4324/9781003569985-1

I develop the notion that Winnicott's theory of defenses against objects operates with all manifestations of defense in the clinical context and that play is a methodology that emerges in the analysis of these defenses.

I also deconstruct how elements of defense analysis operate during the process of play in analytic work. In play, a patient's defense process often involves an experience of aliveness and vividness within the analytic couple and is less oriented toward secondary process metacommentary about defensive function than is typical of more formal defense interpretation. The emergence of the analysis of defense that occurs during play is not meant to challenge other forms of defense analysis but is rather adjacent to these forms of defense analysis. This view of a cluster of approaches to defense analysis is consistent with an emergent theme in this volume (one that I will elaborate a bit later in this introduction), namely that epistemological and ontological approaches often operate simultaneously in analytic work. In Chapter 1, I theorize about defense processes during play and clinically examine these processes in two vignettes.

In Chapter 2, I develop a concept called "the activity of neutrality." It is my view that despite moments of playing and the use of reverie being anything but neutral in the conventional sense of the word, that both Winnicott and Bion were trying to find a better balance between helping patients to know themselves and to experience themselves as alive and creative people. They were suggesting that there are many ways to learn and discover oneself in analysis besides the yield provided by interpretations.

I discuss the analyst's neutrality as an activity: a constantly moving position and an always-evolving process characterized by the analyst's thinking and curiosity about how to help the patient better know and become himself. I explore how neutrality might apply to the play concept since play is characterized by constant transit – transit especially between unrepresented and symbolized experience but also play that involves the transit between various temporal modalities of past, present, and future.

I maintain that neutrality is a cluster concept (Wittgenstein, 1953) that includes a number of functions. I review recent theoretical shifts regarding neutrality and provide an illustrative clinical vignette.

Developing some of the themes of Chapter 2, in Chapter 3, "Playing, Paradox, and Analytic Activity between Knowing and Being," I explore some ways that we help patients to hold paradoxical realities intrinsic to transference and play in analytic work. I suggest that Winnicott's guardianship of the setting for the emergence of playing raises questions about the role of neutrality in an ontological analysis. I try to illustrate some ways that the work of helping patients to hold paradox in play overlaps with a concept that I referred to earlier in Chapter 2 as an "activity of neutrality." I explore how, in the analytic process, understanding and being are two dimensions of the analytic process that work in concert with each other. Often the analyst works quietly in spaces between epistemological and ontological approaches in the holding of paradox.

In Chapter 4, "Winnicott's Paradox of Being with and without Memory and Desire: Notes on a Letter from Winnicott to Bion," I take as my focus a letter that Winnicott wrote to Bion after hearing Bion's lecture "Without Memory and Desire" (Bion, 1967). I use the letter as a taking off place to think about some of the overlap and differences in these two revolutionary thinkers. In certain respects, Winnicott took exception to the concept of "without memory and desire" in that he focused on the analyst as both a symbolic and actual object. He was not entirely willing to dispense with the analyst's memory and desire. I also explore some ways that play and reverie relate to one another at a conceptual and technical level.

I argue that Winnicott's aim was to hold a paradoxical position between the analyst trying to be without memory and desire and trying to be attentive to his intentions as well. Winnicott wanted his patients to experience him in certain ways as an actual object, even as he was giving himself over to the task of not imposing his ideas and directions onto the patient. I suggest that this letter marks an extremely important moment in the history of an ontological approach to psychoanalysis and, more generally, in the history of psychoanalysis.

In Chapter 5, I provide a close reading of Winnicott's (1968) paper, "Playing, Creativity, and the Search for the Self." It is the second leg of Winnicott's two-part opus on play and was published as Chapter 4 in his volume, *Playing and Reality*. I examine Winnicott's revolutionary discovery that play is the logical undergirding of the analytic process itself in connection with how he discusses time and the setting in his clinical paper.

Winnicott's (1968) paper is fundamentally about play and is his most detailed description of play with an adult patient. In many ways, it is also one of his best elaborations of how he regards temporality (Steinbock, 2024; Goldberg, 2024; Cooper, 2024). I suggest that for Winnicott, play always involves time, the loss of time or object, namely what I have referred to as the play of mourning (Cooper, 2023b). For Winnicott, temporality is also inextricably bound with his notion of place, and they are both contained in the analytic setting. This is a setting that allows for the emergence of play and creative experiences of self, in time in general and for the time being. I provide some clinical material to illustrate my interpretation of Winnicott's two major papers on play.

In Chapter 6, I explore my own view of how temporality "plays out" in clinical analysis. Phrases such as "for the time being" and "wasting time" are explored with regard to the intersubjective dimension of analytic work. I try to compare some of these ideas to Winnicott (1968), Loewald (1972), and Laplanche (1997, 1999) regarding temporality in analytic work. I offer a few clinical vignettes to help explore a few concepts related to time, namely "for the time being" and "wasting time."

In Chapter 7, I think about play in the context of working with Oedipal conflicts and unconscious fantasies. There are unique forms of play associated with how Oedipal conflicts emerge in analytic work that I refer to as the

Oedipal citadel. I elaborate on some of the fantasies and defenses that protect some patients in their Oedipal fixations, particularly those related to forms of personal isolation. To some extent, cover-up is intrinsic to Oedipal conflict and fantasy, but what is covered up is quite variable.

In this chapter, I also emphasize elements of personal isolation that the patient cultivates in order to protect love for a desired Oedipal parent and the conscious and unconscious fantasies associated with this love. While the schizoid's isolation tries to solve the problem of fearing that his love destroys, the patients described here use forms of personal isolation to cover up and secure the gratification of Oedipal fantasies. Their isolation also serves to protect them from fantasies of unique forms of destructiveness in relation to self and the desired other. The citadel, a concept from Guntrip's (1969) description of defenses protecting the schizoid patient's fear of destructive love, is characterized here for the neurotic patient as virtual since, in some ways, each of the participants in Oedipal conflict turns a "blind eye" (Steiner, 1985) to a staged cover-up.

Three clinical illustrations examine the process of shifts from turning a blind eye to sustaining a process of seeing what is being covered up but has already been seen. Play emerges during these shifts.

Finally, in Chapter 8, "'Being Careful in Only a Perverse Way': The Use of Aesthetic Experience in Psychoanalytic Work," I offer a personal contribution about my own use of aesthetic experience in clinical work. I view it as a form of play, personal and idiosyncratic to be sure. I mention a few strong personal influences on my thinking in general, such as the painting of Richard Diebenkorn and the poetry of Bob Dylan.

The abstract oil painter Richard Diebenkorn's "Notes to Myself upon Beginning a Painting" were discovered after his death in 1995. These notes remarkably overlap with elements of the ontological analysis of both Winnicott and Bion. I will elaborate on a few elements of analytic listening from inside my own personal "aesthetic matrix," which include my interest in the painting of Richard Diebenkorn, the poetry of Bob Dylan, and a lifelong enjoyment of entomology and fly fishing as it comes into "play" with analytic work. There will be special attention to a few varieties of visual and verbal imagery linked to auxiliary-containing functions for the analyst. I will emphasize the importance for each analyst to make use of their aesthetic experience as a rich resource for expanding the analyst's clinical imagination.

As I mentioned earlier, my exploration of play has led me to a more general consideration of the tensions and complementarity of the dimensions of being and knowing in analytic work.

In thinking about the epistemological and ontological strands of analytic work, I have come to the conclusion that in some ways, we are not well served by thinking about different theories with these descriptions. I say this because some theories are themselves so complex and multidimensional that I have tried to set about on a different task. This is a matter that I explore as an important leitmotif throughout the book.

The project that emerged in writing this book was one in which I tried to begin with the assumption that the knowing and being strands of my analytic work are interwoven. Ogden's (2022) highly original paper, in which he assigned different theorists to these categories, was meant as a scaffolding to help us think about these dimensions. He stated in that paper that, of course, there is overlap and that these characterizations regarding theories can only go so far.

As I thought about these matters in my own work, I considered how Freud might be usefully thought of as a partly ontological thinker. While we associate so many of his discoveries in relation to helping patients to know more about their unconscious minds, relatively early on in his theorizing, he began developing free-floating attention as a way to help himself from thinking too much about the origin of symptoms. He was likely content to think about the origin of the symptoms when he held the hope that it would provide a cure for neurotic symptoms. When he discovered that it didn't, he turned to a new methodology, one in which he was becoming a more subjective participant as he demanded of himself to try for free floating attention. Parsons (2024) has elaborated this theme quite beautifully.

Freud was discovering a new way to be with his patients that might allow them to learn more about themselves and perhaps experience themselves in new ways. In making himself a subject, he was discovering that unless the analyst does so, nothing will happen that we hope for in analytic work.

Similarly, while it is meaningful to think of Winnicott and Bion as the progenitors of ontological elements of analysis, their thinking and practice were varied and multidimensional. In some ways, there are two papers that seem to provide a pure culture of these respective theories along ontological lines. For Winnicott, Chapter 4 of *Playing and Reality*, "Playing, Creativity, and the Search for the Self," described an analysis of a patient in which he very consciously eschews making relatively obvious interpretations and is instead aiming for helping the patient featured in this chapter to experience herself in entirely new ways.

Bion's "Without Memory and Desire" lecture is, for some, his credo regarding clinical technique. Yet we know through reading the body of his work as well as Winnicott's that they each used many of the traditional interpretations that they were trained to use, presumably toward some good end. Some have argued that Bion didn't mean to suggest that the analyst is always without memory and desire (Abram and Hinshelwood, 2023). Instead, Bion was radically shifting the analyst's focus and activity away from a steady thinking process regarding formulation, in some ways staying true to the model of free-floating attention.

As mentioned earlier, in Chapter 4 of this volume, titled "Winnicott's Paradox of Being with and without Memory and Desire: Notes on a Letter from Winnicott to Bion," I discuss a letter that Winnicott wrote to Bion in October 1967 after hearing Bion's lecture on "Without Memory and Desire." In this chapter, I compare playing and reverie as the central metaphors that

Winnicott and Bion respectively used in their body of work. While both Winnicott and Bion were beginning to explore elements of the analyst's actuality in contrast to Klein, Winnicott's objections to Bion's instructions to analysts are crucial in understanding Winnicott's theory of play. I argue that his listening position is not simply to be without memory and desire but to hold that analytic ideal along with his steadfast interest in his own desires and memories as an actual object.

In many ways, play helps each of us as patients and analysts to hold multiple levels of psychic reality, including temporal reality (e.g., Steinbock, 2024; Goldberg, 2024; Cooper, 2024). At the level of our professional engagement with one another, it is also sometimes difficult for our psychoanalysts to hold the multiplicity of theoretical approaches to understanding, the tensions between knowing and being in clinical analysis. Sometimes, in developing theoretical ideas, we oversimplify complex dimensions of theory and minimize how, at the clinical borders, there is much intersection (see Cooper, 2015). This is why I refer to the current state of analysis as "post-pluralistic" (Cooper, 2015).

I often think of Hannah Arendt's (1951) continual observation that tribalism in human beings (and thus including psychoanalysts) is always something to resist, no matter how natural it might feel in particular ways. For psychoanalysts, it's even better to be curious about our own tribalism. It seems to me that certainty and faddism in psychoanalytic thinking and in psychoanalytic group behavior are often chosen as a resistance to uncertainty. It is a great paradox indeed when even theories that feature uncertainty drift toward the wish for certainty.

I hope that some of these essays help us to think about the ways that learning and growing, knowing and being, have proceeded in concert and in tension with each other as psychoanalytic theories have flourished. I would like to think that my way of theorizing play in connection with a number of psychoanalytic phenomena exemplifies an approach, albeit likely idiosyncratic to me, that allows for a way of thinking about the relationship between being and knowing. Finding play with our theories is perhaps another subtheme of the project in this book (e.g., Cooper, 2017). While I have frequently theorized these matters in terms of post-pluralism, I hope that here it is, more than anything, embodied in these essays.

References

Abram, J. and Hinshelwood, R. D. (2023) *The Clinical Paradigns of Donald Winnicott and Wilfred Bion*. London: Routledge.

Arendt, H. (1951) Continental imperialism: The pan movements. In *The Origins of Totalitarianism*. Tribal Nationalism. New York: Harcourt Brace.

Bion, W. (1967) Notes on memory and desire. *Psychoanal. Forum* 2: 272–280.

Cooper, S. H. (2015) Clinical theory at the borders: Emerging and unintended crossings in the development of clinical theory. *Int. J. Psychoanal.* 96: 273–292.

Cooper, S. H. (2017) The analyst's use of theory or theories: The play of theory. *J. Amer. Psychoanal. Assn.* 65: 859–882.
Cooper, S. H. (2018) Playing in the darkness: Use of the object and use of the subject. *J. Amer. Psychoanal. Assn.* 66: 743–764.
Cooper, S. H. (2023a) *Playing and Becoming in Psychoanalysis*. London: Routledge.
Cooper, S. H. (2023b) The play of mourning. *J. Amer. Psychoanal. Assn.* 71: 61–82.
Cooper, S. H. (2024) Playing in time: A discussion of Steinbock's Reflections on "A woman who found she needed a session of indefinite length." *Psychoanalytic Dialogues* 34: 681–687.
Diebenkorn, R. (1995) Notes to myself on beginning a painting. Trudy Montgomery Gallery.
Goldberg, P. (2024) On the discovery/creation of lived time: Discussion of Steinbock. *Psychoana. Dial.* 34: 687–692.
Guntrip, H. (1969) *Schizoid Phenomena, Object Relations, and the Self*. New York: International Universities Press.
Laplanche, J. (1997) The theory of seduction and the problem of the other. *Int. J. Psycho-Anal.* 78: 653–666.
Laplanche, J. (1999) *Essays on Otherness*. London: Routledge.
Loewald, H. (1972) The experience of time. *Psychoanal. St. Child* 27: 401–410.
Ogden, T. (2022) *Coming to Life in the Consulting Room: Toward a New Analytic Sensibility*. London: Routledge
Palmer, J. (2023) The aesthetic matrix: A conversation between a painter and a psychoanalyst. *Psychoanal. Inq.* 44: 327–337.
Parsons, M. (1999) The logic of play. *Int. J. Psychoanal.* 80: 871–884.
Parsons, M. (2024) Practice and praxis: Psychoanalysis as an act of love. *Psychoanal. Q* 93: 219–248.
Steinbock, S. (2024) Reflections on "A woman who found she needed a session of indefinite length": A look at chapter four of Winnicott's Playing and Reality through the prism of its modalities of temporality. *Psychoanal. Dial.* 34: 676–688..
Steiner, J. (1985) Turning a blind eye: The cover up for Oedipus. *Int. Rev. Psychoanal.* 12: 161–172.
Winnicott, D. W. (1959) Ego distortion in terms of true self and false self. In *The Collected Works of D. W. Winnicott*, ed. L. Caldwell and H. T. Robinson, Vol. 6. Oxford: Oxford University Press, pp. 159–174.
Winnicott, D. W. (1967) Letter to W. Bion. In *The Collected Works of D. W. Winnicott*, ed. L. Caldwell and H. T. Robinson, Vol. 8. Oxford: Oxford University Press. pp. 157–158.
Wittgenstein, L. (1953) *Philosophical Investigations*. New York: Macmillan.

1 Living an Experience of Defense

Exploring Defensive Process within the Play Framework

Winnicott's (1960) pivotal observation that some defenses are organized against object failure, in contrast to ego-defenses which titrate anxiety or depressive affect, marked two important shifts in defense theory. First, Winnicott suggested that the referent point for defense was no longer exclusively an impulse but instead an object requiring the individual to be vigilant and protective. Winnicott (1960) implied that this latter type of defense (defense against objects) may overlap with ego-defense organized against id-impulse (Cooper, 1989). He also made it clear that he did not wish to challenge the traditional definitions of defense offered by Freud (1894) or A. Freud (1946) as related to ego-defense organized against id-impulse.

A second feature of Winnicott's (1960) discussion of defense was that it included not only the mechanisms of defense deployed by the patient but also the analyst's experience of the patient's defensive organization, particularly in reference to false self-organization.

I will examine how elements of defense analysis operate during the process of play in analytic work. I suggest that the emergence of the analysis of defense that occurs during play intrinsically relates to "defenses organized against objects" as well as defenses against impulses (Winnicott, 1960). I further suggest that Winnicott's observation that some defenses are organized against objects is a more generally applicable observation about how defenses operate in the analytic couple. In the intersubjective space of how defenses against objects operate, play sometimes emerges, offering new opportunities for observation and experience.

All forms of defense interpretation seek to bring the patient into inner experience that we expend effort to not know about or feel too deeply. As it emerges in analytic work, my focus here is on how play makes these experiences and drive-related reverie emanating from the patient and analyst come alive in a lived experience within the analytic couple.

That play provides another avenue for the analysis of defense is not meant to challenge the efficacy of other forms of defense analysis aimed at, in Winnicott's terms, "ego-defenses against id-impulse" (e.g., Schafer, 1968; Brenner, 1982; Kris, 1982; Gray, 1996). Rather, instances when play emerges in the analysis of defense are adjacent to these other forms of defense analysis. Sometimes play emerges from other, earlier forms of defense interpretation

DOI: 10.4324/9781003569985-2

more related to noting various feelings or impulses that are being avoided or mitigated through defensive operations. The emergence of play in relation to defensive process may provide a new sense of vitality for the patient and is less oriented toward secondary process metacommentary about defensive function than is typical of more formal defense interpretation (e.g., Gray, 1996).

Seeing the de facto analysis of defense during play as operating simultaneously with other modes of defense interpretation is consistent with Ogden's observation (2019, 2022) that epistemological and ontological approaches often operate simultaneously in analytic work. Ogden (2019) suggested that in contrast to the epistemological emphases of Freud and Klein, the work of Bion (1967, 1970) and Winnicott (1968b, 1968c), through different central mediums (dreaming and playing, respectively), emphasized the ontological dimensions of analytic work. Winnicott (1968b) himself noted in his first paper on play and his seminal paper on interpretation in psychoanalysis in the same year (Winnicott, 1968a) that his focus was an ontological one when he stated that he emphasized the experience of play as much or more than the unconscious content that play revealed (e.g., Klein, 1932).

A great deal of defense analysis spanning various theorists of defense such A. Freud (1946), Brenner (1982), Schafer (1968), and Gray (1996), despite some of their theoretical differences, involves considering a defense as a patient's shift away from an idea, affect, or unconscious fantasy that caused anxiety (Cooper, 1989). This approach generally aims to help a patient to enhance observing capacities and thus knowing. While Winnicott never challenged extant theories of defense related to neurotics, his theory development and therapeutic action in certain ways implied some changes in the ways that we think about defenses.

I will begin by describing Winnicott's major contribution to the understanding of defensive process. Then I will examine how my own definitions of play (Cooper, 2018, 2019, 2022, 2023) are situated in relation to Winnicott's (1968b, 1968c) and Parsons's (1999) contributions to play theory. I theorize and try to illustrate how play processes emerge in analytic work and shed light on meaningful shifts in defensive process. Finally, as I link Winnicott's theory of play to the analysis of defense, I will also try to consider how a few other elements of Winnicott's theory development are related to play, particularly his consideration of the capacity to be alone (Winnicott, 1965) and the environment and object mother as components of the "object in the analytic setting" (Green, 1975).

Winnicott's Contribution to the Theory of Defense with Relevance for Play

In Winnicott's (1960) major contribution to defense theory, he offered a pivotal observation that some defenses are organized against object failure, in contrast to neurotic defenses which titrate anxiety or depressive affect. Here

Winnicott marked two shifts in defense theory. First, the reference point for defense was no longer exclusively an impulse. A new referent point was now a person from whom the individual required protection, which may overlap with ego-defense organized against id-impulse (Cooper, 1989).

Winnicott (1945, 1960) was suggesting that some experiences in development prevent the capacity for intrapsychic defenses to mitigate affect flooding. He posited that when the caretaker is so unable to provide holding, either through spurious reality testing, excessive narcissistic preoccupation, or depression, the child learns to defend against objects, not just to mitigate impulses.

A second feature of Winnicott's (1960) discussion of defense was that it included not only the mechanisms of defense deployed by the patient but also both his or her experience and the analyst's experience of the patient's shell. Winnicott was aware that sometimes the patient's deadness is conveyed by the patient and experienced by the analyst. Most importantly, though, this defensive constellation could be seen as having a pervasive impact on the patient's personality, not only a distinct mechanism operating to titrate affect. Winnicott brought us more deeply into a level of experiencing the patient's lack of aliveness and creativity, not just observing a mechanism of defense such as reaction formation against hostility or a denial of a piece of emotional reality.

Winnicott's (1960) bold theoretical contribution to defense placed him squarely with a focus on the object as more than the receptacle of projections. Winnicott's descriptions of the object in this paper on defense, as was true in "Primitive Emotional Development" (Winnicott, 1945) and his transitional object paper (Winnicott, 1953), consistently elaborated on elements of the actuality of the object and the role that the environment plays in the formation of the personality, as has also been detailed by Bonaminio (2012), Aguayo (2018), and Abram and Hinshelwood (2023). For example, Winnicott (1953, p. 17) stated that the importance of the transitional object is its status as a "real," actual object, not only its function as a symbolic one. Winnicott was not only emphasizing the importance of the environment for healthy development but also how the presence of caretakers with depression or narcissistic vulnerability impedes the progress of development (Winnicott, 1945, 1960). In describing how defenses may operate in relation to the actuality of the object, he was beginning to articulate how the psychic work that is done by the child serves to allay both the concerns of the child and of the parent, often at the child's psychic expense.

Winnicott's interest in the actuality of the object has implications for the analyst in the analytic situation, participating and experiencing the patient's defensive organization. Sometimes playing allows for the patient's more vivid experience of their defensive functioning. Playing also sometimes sheds light on elements of previously unanalyzed elements of transference-countertransference, thus helping in what is a de facto interpretation of defense and how the analyst potentially contributes to elements of what has not yet been analyzed.

Winnicott's (1968b) notion of playing as a central metaphor for the therapeutic action of psychoanalysis involved a clustering of elements of the analytic process, including defense, unconscious fantasy, the transference-countertransference matrix, resistance, and repetition. Winnicott (1968c) brought us into a greater level of awareness of what stops us from finding playing, a view from inside an intersubjective process in which defenses play their part.

In introducing the analyst's key responsibilities as bringing the patient to play (the analyst as participant and supervisor of play), Winnicott was implying that defense was now seen as part of the fabric of what permitted and obstructed this process. Winnicott (1945, 1968a, 1968b) began this trend when he described helping patients to "come alive," to feel the creative sparks of their person, and "live" in a place and time (Winnicott, 1945). In addressing the matter of how defenses are addressed through play, I am highlighting the importance of noting that it is often a slightly different kind of lived experience with the analyst that relates to helping patients to better hold paradoxical realities (Parsons, 1999; Cooper, 2018, 2019, 2022, 2023).

Bonaminio (2012, p. 1478) put it well when he said that for Winnicott, "the mind is an organized defense, a pseudo-integration that replaces and holds together a precarious psychic integration; it protects the self from disintegration." Winnicott viewed each of us as a jerry-rigged accumulation of our "bits and pieces" (Winnicott, 1968b), seizing on whatever form of integration is available at any given moment. In fact, for Winnicott, integration itself is a kind of epiphenomenal illusion within psychoanalytic theory.

Winnicott sought to help his patients find their own creative selves, their sense of feeling alive (Winnicott, 1968c). Implicitly this involves the freeing up of impulses and fantasies from the stranglehold of too much emphasis on defensive function. Playing involves entering these defensive constellations, less through a technique that notes what a defense is protecting against and less focused on speaking about a defensive operation. This brings us to a consideration of Winnicott's theory of playing and my own ways of thinking about play so that I might further develop my thesis about the relevance of play to the analysis of defense.

Playing and the Experience of Defense

Winnicott's theory of play related to a general level of describing how psychoanalysis is a form of play. He emphasized the patient's experiences of playing as therapeutic and less the content that play revealed, which had been part of the purview of Klein's (1932) contributions to play in the analysis of children. Winnicott's (1968b) shift of focus from the symbolic meaning of play to the experience of play was summarized in his statement: "I am making a significant distinction between the meaning of the noun, 'play,' and the verbal noun, 'playing'" Winnicott (1968b, pp. 39–40).

Winnicott did not describe how transference, unconscious fantasy, conflict, or defenses are analyzed in play, leaving it to subsequent theorists such as Caper (1996), Parsons (1999), Roussillon (2011), Benjamin (2016), Cooper (2018, 2019, 2021, 2022, 2023), Abram (2021), and Corbett (2022) to describe elements of therapeutic action embedded in play.

Parsons (1999) explored the underlying logic of play in the analytic situation. Parsons argued that play operates to hold paradox, most conspicuously in the operation of transference in which things are both real and not real at the same time. His examples reflect quite beautifully changes in the patient's emergent language or reverie that allow a deeper commentary and experience of transference.

In agreement with Parsons (1999, 2007), I have suggested that in the analysis of adults, playing marks the arrival of new idiomatic or incongruous forms of responsiveness by the patient or analyst through which defenses, transference, or unconscious fantasy may be observed in a slightly new way within the analytic couple (Cooper, 2022, 2023, 2024a, 2024b). I mean by idiomatic that the patient's or analyst's use of even ordinary language might veer into an incongruous phrasing or involve new and creative ways of linking sequestered parts of self, internal objects that live in their own province but are not held accountable in relation to the individual's suffering or their other internal object experiences (Cooper, 2023). As I hope to illustrate here, play can help to hold paradoxical realities that have been warded off or sequestered through defensive processes.

Play sometimes arrives to provide new levels of observation regarding how patients have instituted transference in their analysis, including the ways that defenses organize how the analyst is unconsciously seen and experienced (e.g., Cooper, 2018; 2019; 2021; 2023). This view overlaps with and is influenced by Roussillon's (2011, p. 184) sense that "play is an analyzer of the patient's relationship to the object." Roussillon was interested in how play facilitates symbolization and how play activates particular drive-related impulses in the transference.

The importance of the arrival of idiomatic or incongruous forms of expressiveness also overlaps with Bollas's (1987, 1989) focus on the patient's idiom as an expression of character and of the patient's "true self" (Winnicott, 1960). Bollas (1987, 1989) emphasized the analyst's efforts to find the unique forms of language that arise in patient and analyst that allow for the expression of something new from unconscious experience, or to allow what was obvious but unseen to be seen.

My framework for playing is broad insofar as I believe that playing occurs in relationship to what it reveals both about unconscious fantasy (the content of play) and also through the process of playing in analytic work. As process, playing sometimes occurs when patient and analyst are engaging in new forms of communication, including elements of self-observation and new forms of performative action. Playing emerges from the patient's associations, the analyst's reverie, and new ways of listening "for, to and with" (Reis, 2021) elements of the patient's and analyst's experiences of what has not yet been verbalized or symbolized (e.g., Cooper, 2018, 2019).

For example, a patient who used a great deal of self-sufficiency in relation to his narcissistic mother began using a term to refer to her that seemed like a parapraxis of sorts. He was quite surprised and laughed when he said for the first time in referring to his mother, "My mother, for as long as I have known her." The patient was struck by his unusual phrasing in relation to a parent, as if his language demonstrated to him an even deeper awareness of how much his self-sufficiency operated in his daily life. At one point in his analysis, when he disagreed with me about a billing matter related to a missed session on his part, he nevertheless smiled and referred to me as "my analyst for as long as I have known him." In this moment, something in the patient's defenses against relying on his mother and his analyst came together in his unusual verbal phrasing, providing him a deeper experience of the contorted lengths he went to avoid disappointment by not depending too much on anyone among his intimate relationships.

Here, playing brought into focus a sequestered part of self that exerted control over the patient's needs and wishes. His language demonstrated something being acted out by the patient related to managing his unconscious attachment to his mother. Using that phrase with me also suggested his growing awareness that his needs for me were also threatening. This patient was, for periods of time, unable to hold a paradoxical reality between his wishes to express his needs and be vulnerable on one side and his need to feel in control on the other. The parts of self that I refer to may be separated by defenses such as denial and dissociation, and the emergence of play in analytic work may facilitate a more integrated commerce between the different parts of self within the patient and between patient and analyst. Put still another way, play sometimes provides a way to partner with previously punishing or sequestered objects and find new ways to mourn and thus live (Cooper, 2023). Playing as an activity can sometimes help integrate these various sequestered internalized objects within the individual, "weaving together" our "bits and pieces" (Winnicott, 1968b, 1968c) as it emerges in analytic work.

While Winnicott was not specific about how playing affected defensive organization, I am suggesting that when he describes how analysis promotes the patient's sense of aliveness (Winnicott, 1945, 1960, 1965) and the state of "going on being" (Winnicott, 1949, p. 245, 1965), he is describing a relaxation of defense structure. However, since Winnicott was largely avoiding emphasizing the content of playing, preferring to focus on the experience of playing, it is not surprising that he would not refer to how playing might address defenses organized against particular kinds of affects or impulses.

It seems quite plausible that his description of not being able to play (Winnicott, 1968b, c) reflects how the presence of defenses constricts us, renders us unimaginative, unable to dream or to think. An overreliance on defensive operations is part of a cluster of symptoms that are manifested in either the inability to play or the way that playing is truncated. In parallel, some conflict theorists, such as A. Kris (1982) and Gray (1996), take as their focus the ways that defenses interrupt the process of free association.

Winnicott's formal theorizing about play arrived quite late in his life and can be seen as inevitably overlapping with other central ideas in his body of theoretical work. For example, we might speculate that in playing, the patient can reduce his or her surveillance of what is being expressed and held back toward the "object mother" (Winnicott, 1945) because the patient can trust more the integrity of the "environment mother." This relates to how Winnicott (1960) described instances of object failure which required a child's vigilance to the unpredictability of externality itself. Some versions of play relate to these defenses as they emerge with patients who struggle with the analyst's reliability and presence, such as the patient I mentioned above. Playing is a kind of activity that emerges from the patient's sense of containment, just as it offers greater suppleness in the way that defenses help to hold paradox. The patient's sense of being less vigilant also jibes with a greater capacity to be alone in the presence of the other (Winnicott, 1965).

Those of us interested in analyzing the "logic of play" (Parsons, 1999) run the risk of eviscerating what is so powerful and perhaps even mysterious about the power of play to contribute to analytic process. I believe that understanding how the elements of play function is worth doing not only because of how it contributes to therapeutic action but also because it might also expand our sense of how some other forms of interpretative responsiveness function in analytic work.

In a lived experience of play, the analyst's work may include the affect or impulse that is motivating a patient's use of defense, but it is also experienced by the analyst in the intersubjective context in which it is being expressed. These affective experiences have become a problem within the analytic couple, experienced by each person in the analytic couple. We have countless examples in the literature of analysts trying to find their own reverie in the context of our patient's inability to dream (e.g., Civitarese, 2008a, 2008b). These efforts are adjacent to, but quite different from, the aim of interpretation expressed by Laplanche and Pontalis (1973) that "Interpretation reveals the modes of the defensive conflict, and its ultimate aim is to identify the wish that is expressed by every product of the unconscious" (p. 227).

Thus, I suggest that Winnicott's analysis of defense partly occurs de facto through the finding of play. Play takes us inside defensive configurations as well as unconscious fantasy, often manifested in transference-countertransference that the patient is instituting through repetition in his or her analysis (e.g., Cooper, 2022, 2023).

In playing, we are trying to gain purchase on varieties of repetition that have "played out" between patient and analyst. In doing so, the analyst takes up various affects, but the analyst or patient tends to speak in a register less about the defenses in operation and more directly in a language that emerges from within the analytic couple. A new language is usually being discovered, even when sometimes the words or phrasing have been there all along, obvious but earlier unseen. Again, this version of play relates to Bollas's (1987) suggestion that analysts are required to learn the unique idiom of each patient for expressing his or her inner life.

Consider an extended example related to the defenses of isolation of affect and, to a lesser degree, dissociation. I aim to illustrate how defense is both embedded within various forms of transference-countertransference and may be illuminated in the context of play between patient and analyst. Sometimes, forms of playing provide added entry points to defensive operations in the analytic couple. Play sometimes interrupts a patient's characteristic or routinized defense or the analyst's routinized interpretive response, allowing a deeper experience of the patient's defensive operations.

Case Vignette: M

Despite her intelligence, sense of humor, and general attractiveness, M could sometimes be quite dull. As the director of the creative department in a software engineering firm, she often made her work sound anything but creative. We began with once-weekly treatment for six months, increased it to twice a week, and then after a year, we began meeting four times a week, at which she began using the couch. The material that I present here is from the period immediately preceding her decision to increase her time and to begin using the couch.

Among some of the most interesting things about M was that despite our having set up a time to meet each week at the same time, during the first six months of our time together and then two times a week for the next six months, M often acted as though we weren't planning on meeting. She would check in with me shortly before our appointed time and ask whether we were meeting. I tried to understand this internally along the lines that she wasn't sure whether I would remember her. At one point when I raised it with her, she followed my line of thought and considered it a plausible understanding, but she didn't resonate with it strongly. M couldn't really elaborate on why it was difficult to hold on to the idea that we had a regular appointment time, but she was curious about it. Something created a sense of uncertainty.

M would describe being frustrated with the CEO and CFO of her company because they unrealistically expected refinements in design or products on a timetable that jibed with their schedules but not with the creative tempo of her team. These conversations with the upper management of her company made her anxious, and she had fantasies of quitting during these intervals.

During these sessions, M presented with a desultory sense of resignation and frustration. She saw no way out, and her associations were sparse and often truncated. Her inner life seemed to boil down to the feeling that she could find no solution to feeling trapped by the demands of her job.

M was the youngest of four siblings and felt responsible for her parents, who had immigrated to the US to improve their lot. Her parents were both highly educated and had had successful careers but had made professional sacrifices to immigrate. M carried a burden of guilt about her parents' sacrifices in ways that she was beginning to become aware of in our work.

I would notice that M would repeatedly come into her sessions and begin talking about something that had potential for feeling alive – something she'd read, music she'd heard, an experience of sex, or conversation that she'd had with her husband – and then it would turn into something stripped of vitality. I kept thinking about the beginning sessions when she didn't know that we had a clearly established appointment. Now, during the first year of our, first, once- and, later, twice-weekly meetings, I felt her disappearing. I also noticed quite remarkably that when I would lay out my calendar for the week, I would sometimes overlook her appointment and come to it only later in recording my schedule (I still schedule using a written appointment book method). I was now, again, not recording her in some way that was the case when we began our work together.

The following summary of a session was noteworthy because it marked what we both saw as a turning point in her decision to see me more frequently in analysis. M came most alive to herself and to me in this session when she stopped herself in a story about a friend, L, whom she had frequently mentioned before. Whenever she had previously talked about L, she had reminded me of who L was and how she knew her. It was always notable because I had long before registered who her friend was to M and was internally curious about why she needed to remind me. This time, as she started to elaborate about L, who was already quite familiar to me, she said, "I feel anxious. I started to remind you of L, but I am pretty sure that you might already know who she is. I feel myself not wanting to take the chance."

What is so interesting here is that M is shifting registers in contrast to her frequent isolation of affect (e.g., stripping an idea or event of its feeling) in the way she often elaborated events. She is also shifting from her usual way of titrating anxiety related to how I would not see or remember her (by showing me again and again what was already obvious or her repeatedly checking in about her appointment times when we began working together).

M is beginning a play process here. She is beckoning herself with a demand to trust that I will remember her. She is becoming aware that she is noticing her faithless elaboration of L's identity. She is trying to hold paradox in a slightly different way. She can simultaneously hold the wish to assume that I would remember her friend (or M's appointment time) while holding and not acting on the wish to make certain that I won't forget L by reminding me of her.

In my view, she is bringing us into a form of play where before it had been unavailable to her in this effort to hold paradox and mutually contradictory wishes. She had historically been enacting and performing her defensive operations on several levels. At the level of isolation of affect, she had been relaying stories stripped of vitality and affect in general. At an intersubjective level, M had reminded me early on of our appointment times. Finally, M had repeatedly reminded me about the identity of a friend in her life when I already knew who this person was (also involving a kind of implicit devaluation of me for not remembering). I am also aware that I had been working internally on my predilection to overlook M in my recollecting her for noting my scheduling.

I regard her interruption of these familiar, routinized actions as a form of playing in the sense that she is introducing a new, risky, unusual turn in her way of participating with me. She interrupted a characteristic defense that newly allowed M and me to explore her experiences more deeply and mine of her defensive operations. M abruptly (or what seemed abrupt) changed the rules of our transference-countertransference engagement in this moment by risking that I already did recall who her friend was. I mean by M's "rules" that she had unconsciously projected onto me a foundational experience from childhood that I would not remember the characters in her life and her as a character (e.g., Symington, 1983).

I also regard M's shift as a form of play because she is making a new effort to hold paradox two seemingly incompatible realities at the same time. On one side, she lacks faith that I will remember who L is, while also knowing that I likely do recall who L is in relation to M.

Quite uncharacteristically, I said to M something at this point that had come into my mind in recent sessions as a fantasy. I had been worried that if I just said it, it might come across as being impatient or hostile. I had been silently translating this fantasy, but I had a different feeling now, perhaps because M was stopping herself and bringing us to a point of play. I said, "A few times I have had a thought that you might come in one day and tell me some basic identifying characteristics about yourself, like that you are married, that you have a daughter, and work as a creative/tech person." M became sad, covered only faintly by a smile. M said that she felt her task in her family was to be not seen and not heard, not a new observation but one that she had lived out with me in this moment of wanting to be seen and feeling the impulse to protect herself through unnecessary reminders of who L was. M's faint smile that was covering her sadness seemed like the bodily recognition of the way that she disappeared and covered up. She was showing us her faithlessness regarding her conviction that she could be noticed and recognized as sad.

In relating to M a kind of fantasy of mine, I was following up on her self-reflection regarding a cluster of defensive processes, including isolation of affect, denial, and undoing. I was speaking to her from a place of deep experience. First, I was relating a fantasy about M, a partial picture of how she resides inside my mind and how my imagination is triggered by our work together. There is some aggression that is being brought back to her and risk. My comment makes conspicuous the violence that she engages in toward herself through her disappearance. There is also aggression marked by the unusual way that I am trying to examine who she is and what she does to herself.

I have spoken to my patient with an exaggerated version of the patient's defense in order to underscore her use of defense. I have in some way described myself in the role that the patient's defensive operations have cast me, namely as having no memory of what she has said. In this imaginative activity on the part of the analyst, we engage in a form of playing which nearly always involves imaginative activity. In some sense, I am working more directly with the patient's ascriptions within her defensive operations. We could liken it to the analyst asking a patient the question when she acts as if he doesn't recall people she has mentioned frequently: "What is it like to feel that I wouldn't remember?" Here though, a new idiom emerges, less organized around that form of secondary process language and, instead, more embedded in the analyst's imagination as conveyed to the patient.

I am also taking on at least two forms of risk with M. First, by engaging in a kind of postured glibness, an exaggeration of the lengths to which she will go to deny that I know her and things about her, lest she be disappointed that I won't remember who she is. I have hopefully not been so glib that it would prevent her from experiencing me as a caring and containing presence as I reveal a kind of thinking and dreaming about her. My guess is that my freedom to let M know about my imaginings was in concert with her own perception of the lengths to which she went to not trust that I would remember important people and events in her life.

Second, in my expressed fantasy to her, a dream or nightmare of sorts, I am verbalizing something about the experiences that I have taken in about our history together. I am describing my experience of how she removes herself in relation to herself and from me. I am silently also considering whether I have been aggressive toward her as a retaliation for constantly being treated as the forgetter or neglecter.

In relaying my fantasy of what I had thought about saying to her, I am conveying in strong form that she occupies a place in my mind. Thus, I must consider my unconscious motivation to establish myself in her mind as someone who can remember her and take her in. This form of posteriori self-reflection about my intervention and the matter of whether it serves to deepen the analysis is a part of what I have referred to as an "ethic of play" (Cooper, 2021). My concerns are partly allayed by the sense that, if anything, this clinical moment brought M into a deeper sense of the cost of her psychic efforts to not presume anything of me in the transference.

M and I began speaking in subsequent sessions more about her anxiety that I would not remember things about her, but now she was interrupting the impulse to state oft-repeated things she had said to identify the characters in her life. I spoke to her about a wish that she had to be found, seen, and heard within her family and me, but that it was so risky to allow me the chance to find her. She said that "even now, I feel something about being found that is different for me. I am relieved to be talking to you about this, not that I feel found but to talk about not being found. When I met my husband, I felt found but I kept disappearing from him when we had nice experiences together after meeting. I would push him away and lie to him about being unavailable. I even broke up with him twice when I didn't really want to, but I thought it would be better than him leaving me. Then I started to trust him."

This is a condensed example of how a form of defensive isolation of affect (stripping her experiences of vitality) was also expressed in the transference-countertransference through my experiences of her disappearing. I felt the pain of her need to unnecessarily remind me of already familiar information, but I also felt the eradication of my person as a remembering, engaged analyst. She was creating me as a familiar object who would not see or hear her while also bringing me closer to her experience of not being seen or heard. Of course, this is the very definition of transference, a selective perception or fantasized elaboration of the analyst in accord with early experience.

In the likely enactment of my not recalling her in my calendar preparation and my boredom, I was feeling the effects of her isolation of affect and her intersubjectively determined disappearance. A efensive covering, the citadel as it were, covered her wishes that I would remember (Cooper, 2024b). In this enactment, I am playing out a particular response to the drive-related impulses that she is expressing through her absenting herself from me (e.g.,Roussillon, 2011). My own work to understand my forgetting her and my boredom involved my own reactions to her defensive processes.

In a sense, M and I began to live a defensive process together, or, put more accurately, we were putting words to how we had already been doing so. It is also an instance of how sometimes defenses against impulses and defenses against objects operate in concert with one another. I was introduced to M's rules of engagement, rules in which we were not to presume a relational history, one in which recording and remembering each other were off-limits. These rules may be considered overlapping with what Symington (1983) referred to as the family's corporate motto. Symington suggested that each patient institutes their family's corporate motto as a part of transference and that patient and analyst form an intersubjective engagement in relation to transference-countertransference. Together, we were incrementally living and communicating from inside some of those transference-countertransference rules of engagement.

Concluding Thoughts

I have suggested that the analyst's responsiveness to the patient's defensive organization during forms of play is adjacent to the more secondary process language of interpretations about defense. Sometimes play emerges from the use of the types of defense interpretation emphasized by theorists such as A. Kris (1982) or Gray (1996). Each form of understanding defenses and communicating with patients regarding their defensive organization is essential.

An obvious element of living an experience of defense is that there are always experiential implications of defense process for both patient and analyst. For patients, often their affective experience of defense process is one of mitigating or replacing an affect with another affect or idea. As analysts, we each listen to a defense such as intellectualization or reaction formation, and it creates unique responses to the particularities of transference-countertransference with a specific patient. Additionally, as psychoanalysis deepens, sometimes the psychic activities of playing and reverie permit us to address the defense surface in a more participatory way.

For example, in my reverie, I entered M's defensive denial of her importance to me in a slightly new way. In my reverie, I recruited her into performing an even more exaggerated version of what she was living in her analysis. In other words, in my reverie, I was even more like a stranger to M than she had already been making me into. I was continuing to experience her hiding and disappearance in relation to her own longings. Now, though, I was feeling and articulating my experience of her disappearance and the implicit eradication of my memory and presence as her analyst. My fantasy, in some ways, emanates from a deep element of countertransference about being not seen in certain ways that mirrored how M felt she would not be seen by me.

In a sense, as I conveyed this exaggerated version of M's sense of not being seen, I was performing this lived experience of being her analyst with her. One could also argue that I was performing an element of role-responsiveness (Sandler, 1976) or projective identification since I was expressing elements of her own experience of not being seen.

Of course, there are other concepts from Winnicott's vast theory development besides play that relate to a patient's capacity to relax defenses, particularly the capacity to be alone in the presence of the other. For example, it is noteworthy that Winnicott (1965, 1968b) explicitly links playing with the capacity to be alone. When M is able to note that she thinks that I already know who her friend is, she is trying to be alone in the presence of the other, her analyst. She does not need as much to manipulate the object/analyst through omnipotent control but instead is allowing for the separateness of the object. As I have tried to make clear, playing, the capacity to be alone, and the relaxation of vigilance to the threatening object often occur in a simultaneous fashion. Here, playing mobilizes the drive-related impulses in the transference, as she is in transit from manipulation of the object (attempts at omnipotent control) to allowing for me as a separate object. This overlaps with Roussillon's (2011, p. 184) statement that in play, "the object is freed of the burden of the use of the object in the process of symbolization."

Winnicott repeatedly described play with reference to "creativity," "coming together," and "relaxation" (Winnicott, 1968b, 1968c). He ends the second of his two-part opus on play (Winnicott, 1968c), largely a clinical case, with the following passage.

> The patient had asked a question and I stated "that the answer to the question could take us to a long and interesting discussion, but it was the question that interested me. You had the idea to ask that question."
>
> Then she said slowly, with deep feeling: "Yes, I see, one could postulate the existence of ME as easily from the question as from the searching."
>
> She had now made the essential interpretation in that the question arose out of what can only be called her creativity, creativity that was a coming together after relaxation, which is the opposite of integration. (p. 64)

Note that here, Winnicott is implying that at times, such as in the false self (Winnicott, 1965), integration is a defense, a pretending that this patient had developed an expertise in because of early experience. The defense relaxes through play. His entire paper is about play and the use of illusion regarding even the length of a session so that time itself is a subject of play in this analysis (Cooper, in press-a). Winnicott is citing the patient's new awareness as a demonstration of play, embedded in the paradox that in the searching itself she is finding something and being found by her analyst.

It is also important to note that my examination of the lived experience of defense within the intersubjective context of analysis does not challenge the idea that defenses are an enduring characterological feature of the individual. Many of us tend to use characteristic defenses across interpersonal situations. A patient who characterologically uses isolation of affect in a variety of contexts might not always be employing that defense in the course of analytic work. It is notable and hopefully productive when or when not the patient is using that defense with his or her analyst at any moment. Play is just one of the ways that patients and analysts discover how to examine and live an experience of defensive process.

I find living an experience of defense with a patient through various forms of finding play, that in turn include using reverie, the arrival of patients, or our own idiosyncratic language, and a posteriori reflection about our participation, to be among the most enlivening parts of doing analytic work. It helps patients to feel and see their defensive functioning in the context of the analytic relationship. Thus, over time, patients also often experience the analyst's experience of their defensive function.

Playing has been but one of the ways that psychoanalysts have tried to interrogate Freud's (1914) revolutionary observation that before the transference can be verbally expressed, it must be enacted. When Winnicott issued his assessment that psychoanalysis is a form of playing, he implicitly and explicitly included the analyst within an intersubjective context for understanding defensive process. Defenses, a lynchpin of internal homeostasis and essential to survival and health, were also now understood as residing inside a larger intersubjective fabric. As we observe and work with defenses, we sometimes have the opportunity to do so from the inside out.

References

Abram, J. (2021) *The Surviving Object: Psychoanalytic Essays on Psychic Survivial of the Object* (New Library of Psychoanalysis). London: Routledge.

Abram, J. and Hinshelwood, R. D. (2023) *The Clinical Paradigms of Donald Winnicott and Wilfred Bion*. New York: Routledge.

Aguayo, J. (2018) Winnicott, Melanie Klein, and W. R. Bion: The controversy over the nature of the external object-holding and container/contained (1941–1967). *Psychoanal. Q.* 87: 767–807.

Benjamin, J. (2016) From enactment to play: Metacommunication, acknowledgement, and the third of paradox. *Rivista Di Psicoanalisi.* 62: 565–593.

Bion, W. (1967) Notes on memory and desire. *Psychoanal. Forum* 2: 272–280.

Bion, W. (1970) *Attention and Interpretation*. London: Karnac Books.

Bollas, C. (1987) *The Shadow of the Object*. London: Free Association Books.

Bollas, C. (1989) *Forces of Destiny*. London: Free Association Books.

Bonaminio, V. (2012) On Winnicott's clinical innovations in the analysis of adults. *Int. J Psycho-Anal.* 93: 1475–1485.

Brenner, C. (1982) *The Mind in Conflict*. New York: International Universities Press.

Caper, R. (1996) Play, experimentation and creativity. *Int. J. Psycho-Anal.* 77: 859–869.

Civitarese, G. (2008a) Caesura as Bion's discourse on method. *Int. J. Psycho-Anal.* 89: 1123–1143.

Civitarese, G. (2008b) Immersion versus interactivity and analytic field. *Int. J. Psycho-Anal.* 89: 279–298.

Cooper, S. H. (1989) Recent contributions to the theory of defense: A comparative view. *J. Amer. Psychoanal Assn* 37: 865–891.

Cooper, S. H. (2018) Playing in the darkness: Use of the object and use of the self. *J. Amer. Psychoanal. Assn* 60: 743–765.

Cooper, S. H. (2019) A theory of the setting: The transformation of unrepresented experience and play. *Int. J. Psycho-Anal.* 100: 1439–1454.

Cooper, S. H. (2021) Toward an ethic of play. *The Psychoanal. Q* 90: 373–397

Cooper, S. H. (2022) The activity of neutrality. *The Psychoanal. Q* 91: 355–369.

Cooper, S. H. (2023) The play of mourning. *J. Amer. Psychoanal. Assn* 71: 61–82.

Cooper, S. H. (2024a). Playing in time: A discussion of Smadar Steinbock's "A look at chapter four of Winnicott's playing and reality through the prism of its modalities of temporality". *Psychoanalytic Dialogues* 34: 689–697.

Cooper S. H. (2024b) The virtual Oedipal citadel: Varieties of isolation, Oedipal conflict, and cover-up. *Journal of the American Psychoanal. Assn.* 72(4): 613–635.

Corbett, K. (2022). Play changes us: Playing the object, becoming the analyst. *J Am Psychoanal Assoc.* 70(2): 263–282.

Freud, A. (1946) *The Ego and the Mechanisms of Defense*. London: International Universities Press.

Freud, S. (1894) The neuropsychoses of defense. *SE* 3: 41–61.

Freud, S. (1914) Remembering, repeating, and working through (further recommendations on the technique of psychoanalysis). *SE* 12: 145–156.

Gray, P. (1996) Undoing the lag in the technique of conflict and defense analysis. *Psychoanal Study Child* 51: 87–101.

Green, A. (1975) The analyst, symbolization, and absence in the analytic setting (on changes in analytic practice and analytic experience) – in memory of D. W. Winnicott. *Int J. Psych-Anal.* 56: 9–22.

Klein, M. (1932) *The Psycho-Analysis of Children*. Rev. edn. London: Hogarth Press and the Institute of Psycho-Analysis, 1949.

Kris, A. (1982) *Free Association*. New Haven, CT: Yale University Press.

Laplanche, J. and Pontalis, J. B. (1973) *The Language of Psychoanalysis*. New York: Norton.

Ogden, T. (2019) Ontological psychoanalysis or "What do you want to be when you grow up?" *Psycho. Q.* 88: 661–684.

Ogden, T. (2022) *Coming to Life in the Consulting Room: Toward a New Analytic Sensibility*. London: Routledge.

Parsons, M. (1999) The logic of play in psychoanalysis. *Int. J. Psycho-Anal.* 80(5): 871–884.

Parsons, M. (2007) Raiding the inarticulate: The internal analytic setting and listening beyond countertransference. *Int. J. Psycho-Anal.* 88(6): 1441–1456.

Reis, B. (2021) The analyst's listening: For, to, with. *Int. J. Psycho-Anal.* 102: 219–235.

Roussillon, R. (2011) *Primitive Agony and Symbolization*. London: Karnac.

Sandler, J. (1976) Countertransference and role-responsiveness. *Int. Rev. Psychoanal.* 30: 43–47.

Schafer, R. (1968) The mechanisms of defense. *Int. J. Psycho-Anal.* 49: 49–67.

Symington, N. (1983) The analyst's act of freedom as agent of therapeutic change. *Int. Rev. Psycho-Anal* 10: 283–291.

Winnicott, D. W. (1945) Primitive emotional development. In *Through Paediatrics in Psychoanalysis,* ed. D. W. Winnicott. New York: Basic Books, 1958, pp. 145–156.

Winnicott, D. W. (1949). ed. Mind and its relation to the psyche-soma. In *Through Paediatrics to Psychoanalysis*. New York: Basic Books, 1958, pp. 243–254.

Winnicott, D. W. (1953). Transitional object and transitional phenomena. *Int. J. Psycho-Anal*, 34: 89–97.

Winnicott, D. W. (1958) The capacity to be alone. *Int. J. Psycho-Anal.* 39: 416–420.

Winnicott, D. W. (1960) ed. Ego distortion in terms of True Self and False Self. In *The Maturational Processes and the Facilitating Environment*. New York: International Universities Press, 1965, pp. 140–152.

Winnicott, D. W. (1965) *The Maturational Processes and the Facilitating Environment*. New York: International Universities Press.

Winnicott, D. W. (1968a) Interpretation in psycho-analysis. In *The Collected Works of D. W. Winnicott: Volume 8,* ed. L. Caldwell and H. T. Robinson. Oxford: Oxford University Press, 2016, pp. 253–257.

Winnicott, D. W. (1968b) *Playing: A Theoretical Statement. Playing and Reality*. London: Tavistock.

Winnicott, D. W. (1968c) *Playing, Creativity, and the Search for the Self. Playing and Reality*. London: Tavistock.

2 The Activity of Neutrality

Our evolving understanding of the complex intersubjectivity that undergirds the analytic situation has raised inevitable questions about the utility of the term "neutrality" as a technical ideal. A joke, a dead serious one, about the impossibility of neutrality might go something like this: We're standing at the crossroads between being too stimulating or too distant, too much an old object or too much a new object, too transparent or too detached, too immersed in the patient's psychic reality versus attempting to be too objective; let's hope that we make the right choice.

The joke addresses a number of principles and tensions that are precious to us as analysts. Neutrality is not a corrupt ideal as long as we can continue to elaborate on what it might mean and how it might be useful. We cannot find a way out of the need to come to these determinations in clinical work.

I will suggest that neutrality is an *activity* on the part of the analyst, a verb rather than a noun. It is not a statically achievable state but instead an always-evolving process. The process of neutrality features, front and center, the analyst's thinking and curiosity about how to help a patient to better know and become himself. It also features the analyst's process of a posteriori self-reflection about inevitable enactment and where the analytic couple finds itself. Whether it is well-named and whether we can find a better term is a matter that I will close with.

As an activity, neutrality suggests a constantly moving, working position. As an activity, it includes the need to scrutinize our belief, or perhaps fantasy, that we can be perfectly poised between different elements of the patient's personality or within our intersubjective engagement with the patient. Yet as an activity, neutrality maintains an appreciation for the value in trying to find optimal positions from which to listen and speak to patients about what they are communicating.

Activity implies dedication, a practice of correction and recovery. This formulation of neutrality is in line with Wilson's (2013) more general notion that countertransference is not a noun but an activity. Similarly, Susan Isaacs (1948) implied many years ago that transference was beneficially understood as an activity of transferring.

I view the activity of neutrality as best understood as a kind of ethic in our practice (Civitarese, 2013; Cooper, 2021). Yet neutrality should not be

DOI: 10.4324/9781003569985-3

fundamentally defined with regard to our ethical guidelines, such as the requirement of abstinence, since it is a clinically refined, subtle, and deeply elusive concept. Neutrality as an ethic involves a commitment to curiosity and self-reflection. Abstinence is a precondition, a necessary but not sufficient element of neutrality.

As we think about neutrality in contemporary psychoanalysis, we are required to think of it as always issuing from a deeply subjective experience of the analyst, a position within the intersubjective space between patient and analyst. We can think about it in advance of our participation and in a posteriori manner about what has occurred, but it is an activity that always implies more, continuing activity. It is in this ongoing effort that the activity of neutrality is an essential element of the analyst's experience of the depressive position (Cooper, 2016).

I believe that this way of thinking of neutrality is compatible with the models of playing (Winnicott, 1968b) and reverie (Bion, 1970). In playing, there is always transit – transit between unrepresented and symbolized experience; between old and new object experiences; and in new, emergent transference-countertransference experience. While moments of play on a moment-to-moment basis are rarely thought of as neutral in the traditional sense of the term, in my view, Winnicott and Bion were each in their own way elaborating clinical sensibilities that addressed what they regarded as a hypertrophied reliance on secondary process language and interpretation. In some ways, the activity of playing was an attempt to be neutral regarding not getting ahead of where our patients are with regard to integrating our understandings and formulations. Winnicott's formulation of playing as the underlying logic of analysis was deeply respectful of Freud's (1914) observation that the transference cannot be expressed before it is enacted.

A Brief Sketch of Recent Contributions to the Neutrality Concept

Contemporary forms of psychoanalysis make the concept of neutrality more challenging to define, yet by no means dispensable. Versions (sometimes caricatures) of analysts attempting to maintain an image of opaque neutrality are far less prominent than they were even 30 years ago in psychoanalytic writing and practice.

In 1996, I stated that for many years, the analyst's capacity for neutrality had been equated in some ways with Aristotle's notion of the "unmoved mover" (Cooper, 1996). In some ways, the term neutrality implied that the analyst could function as a human gyroscopic device, providing stability or direction in navigating clinical processes. But by the mid-1980s, psychoanalysts had widely come to understand that our capacities for regulating our emotional and cognitive abilities to listen and respond were never a steady state, and that in fact, our unsteadiness was itself a subject of interest in making use of our countertransference activity.

Several major shifts have occurred in theory development regarding neutrality in the last 35 years as the intersubjective dimension of psychoanalysis has become better appreciated. One shift involves the understanding that attempts at a neutral stance are not intrinsically tied to restraint on the part of the analyst, despite the fact that there is considerable restraint required in being a psychoanalyst. Immersion in a patient's story is necessary, and enactment is inevitable. We have realized that neutrality, in its most extreme forms of sterility as a construct within our theory of technique, likely involved a wish that we could be more objective as we understand our patients.

Second, we had come to see that each patient and each analytic couple is unique, requiring the analyst to be flexible in approximating what a stance of neutrality might involve with each patient. Anna Freud's (1936) well-known notion of a neutral interpretation poised equidistantly between id, ego, and superego to some extent implied that the determination of this calculus would be unique with each patient. Greenberg (1986) extended Anna Freud's (1936) concept of neutrality to the interpersonal realm, arguing that we must try to find a balanced and equidistant position among the contending dimensions of the patient's personality. Greenberg (1986) suggested that neutrality embodies the goal of establishing an optimal tension between the patient experiencing the analyst as an old and new object.

Like Greenberg's extension of Anna Freud, Kris (1990) also developed the notion of neutrality as patient-based. Focusing on the importance of self-criticism, Kris articulated a notion of functional neutrality to suggest that the analyst must be aware that some patients will feel criticized or blamed, rather than understood, by their interpretation. He also noted that the analyst's reserve might be more likely to be experienced as his criticism or dislike for the patient. Kris was expanding the notion that neutrality is not static but instead requires of the analyst a level of self-reflection about assessing what types of responsiveness will best promote the free associative process.

In parallel, from a contemporary Kleinian perspective, John Steiner (1994) described what he referred to as patient-centered versus analyst-centered interpretation. Steiner (1994) suggested that some personality-disordered patients who are prone to feel criticized, shamed, or paranoid are better able to listen to "analyst-centered" interpretations than "patient-centered" interpretations. He suggested that the analyst be sensitive to the patient's propensity to feel overly responsible for what happens in the transference and to feel persecuted by interpretations that begin with what the patient is psychically doing or expressing. Steiner proposed that by instead making interpretations that concentrate on the patient's view of the analyst, the analyst can help the patient feel safer and take in the content of interpretation.

We see that Greenberg, Kris, and Steiner make an attempt to think about neutrality not simply as a technically defined and prescribed position but rather as a loose scaffolding of sorts that can be applied to the special requirements of particular patients' vulnerabilities or strengths. This kind of clinical sensibility has become integrated into most schools of psychoanalytic thought in ways that I cannot elaborate here (e.g., Mitchell, 2000; Civitarese, 2008).

A general understanding of the intersubjective roots of analytic work requires us to stretch our definitions of neutrality to include the notion that patients' understandings of themselves are constructed and symbolized not only by words themselves but by the ways that words come to mark the relational context in which they emerge. If interpretation is a form of object relation, as emphasized by both Ogden (1994) and Bromberg (1998), then the analyst must take into account that for patients to learn about themselves through the analyst's observations, there is a simultaneous reality, one in which the patient is often experiencing the analyst's personal responsiveness (Hoffman, 1983; Aron, 1991).

In order for a patient to better understand or be with himself and to examine more particularly what is being repeated and enacted in analysis, they must feel either a level of freedom or awareness of their resistance to freedom in examining the analyst's responsiveness. Renik's (1996) critique of the "perils of neutrality" was largely a renunciation of a model of neutrality that minimized both the analyst's affective participation as well as the patient's often exquisite awareness of his participation.

It is unfortunate, though, that the construct of spontaneity has been juxtaposed as opposite to neutrality. What appears to be analytic spontaneity in some sense always arises out of a shared relational history and is itself a property of the intersubjective field. *Spontaneity is itself a kind of shared illusion between patient and analyst.*

I believe that even when analysts are using more prescribed techniques, there are subtle shifts going on within the analyst that involve trying to find reverie, trying to find new forms of containment, or patience and curiosity with what they are hearing. So, the kinds of things that we call spontaneity, for quite understandable reasons, are often more conspicuous but not always more original or creative than elements of quiet work going on under the surface that have given rise to the moments we refer to as spontaneous.

In evaluating the activity of neutrality, it matters that there are different types of activity implied in Bionian, Winnicottian, Ego Psychological and Relational models that go beyond what I can address here. Briefly, though, it obviously matters whether, how, and to what degree the analyst allows his clinical imagination to roam as another voice in the analytic setting. Civitarese (2008, p. 177) has emphasized the necessity for the analyst to be immersed at multiple levels of content and form in what patients are conveying. He elaborates on Bion's concern that we can prematurely arrive at meaning by reminding us that neutrality is important as a "sweet fruit of skepticism" (Barthes, 1970, p. 37). This meaning of skepticism revolves less around doubt and more around meanings central to neutrality, such as observation and reflection.

For a moment, consider when Freud introduced the notion of free-floating attention in his letter to Fliess (Freud, 1954). Freud stated in relation to his patient Herr E. that,

> I adopted the expedient of renouncing working by conscious thought, so as to grope my way further into the riddles only by blind touch. Since I started this, I have been doing my work, perhaps more skillfully than before, but I do not really know what I am doing." (pp. 311–2)

Here, Freud has trust in his own mind, allowing that he will not know in advance how he might interpret what Herr E. conveys.

This kind of trust overlaps with but is also different from the kind of trust that Winnicott (1968a, 1968b) stated in the notion of waiting for his patients to come to their own understanding of what they were saying. It is also overlapping with Winnicott's dedication to helping patients find play in relation to their inner lives. Something that every approach in psychoanalysis suggests, though, is a process of trust, curiosity, and scrutinization of how we are thinking and feeling about what our patients are communicating. These processes comprise the activity of neutrality.

Neutrality as Process and Activity

I think of neutrality as a "cluster" concept (Wittgenstein, 1953), a concept that includes a number of functions and is defined from the context and cultures in which they are employed. Neutrality includes the analyst's continual process of self-reflection. It includes the analyst's thinking before making an interpretation or asking a question, as he listens to the patient's associations, and as he is thinking retrospectively about what is being enacted in particular moments of analytic work. In this view, neutrality is a cluster of ideas that operate simultaneously to form a never achievable ideal of practice. Wittgenstein's (1953) notion of a cluster concept is one that is defined by a weighted list of criteria such that no single one of these criteria is either necessary or sufficient for membership.

As a group of functions, we may say that neutrality involves an attempt to maintain a non-judgmental attitude toward all of the patient's wishes, fantasies, and feelings. I also think of neutrality as a dedication to working with the analyst's subjective experience and points of view, and to abstain from immediate judgment of his own thoughts and feelings. Neutrality is a form of "countertransference activity" (Wilson, 2013) featuring the analyst's self-reflection about where the analytic couple has been and why. At the center of this question is the requirement that the concept incorporate the necessary immersion from which an ideal of neutrality may emerge.

Neutrality also implies a kind of preconscious clinical and moral compass, a guardianship of the mindfulness intrinsic to analytic work. This guardianship suggests that the analyst's activity is different with each patient and is in a constant state of disequilibrium. These activities are also a way to describe, in simple language, the notion of Winnicott's holding environment or Bion's concept of container-contained.

It seems to me that at this point in understanding the analyst's participation in the analytic process, the cluster must also include neutrality as an unconscious fantasy by the analyst of an ideal responsiveness. In other words, what makes a cluster concept such as neutrality uniquely psychoanalytic is that it must also involve its inevitable, freighted, unconscious meaning. Having said that, so much has occurred in theory development to alert us to the enigmatic blend of immersion and distance that accompanies any form of analytic responsiveness.

The concept of neutrality involves a set of ideals to strive for, but the term itself is, I believe, obfuscating because it is too embedded in a model of psychoanalysis that developed prior to our understanding of enactment as ubiquitous. The term also developed prior to our understanding that, as Civitarese (2008) puts it, "After all, truth slips away at the moment when one thinks one has pinned it down" (p. 176). If interpretation as a linguistic act inevitably involves the enactment of unconscious process through the content of what is being expressed, then the quest for truth itself is always in process. The analyst is never in an ideal listening position except in the process of a posteriori reflection on what has occurred. In fact, this process of reflection about meaning, about being with the patient (Winnicott, 1968a; Ogden, 2024), and about the inevitability of enactment marks the activity of neutrality as a vital dimension of the analyst's experience of the depressive position (Cooper, 2016).

In recent years, there has likely been more emphasis on retrospective thinking about where we have been with a patient, including where our enactments have led us. In contrast, the following clinical example relates to the activity of neutrality of a more subtle nature, featuring aspects of neutrality that overlap with the analyst's self-reflection during the process of interpretation. One could say that it involves the analyst's holding or "waiting," a quite active process as Winnicott (1968a) described it.

In *The Piggle,* Winnicott (1977) emphasized in his work with Gabrielle, his two-and-a-half-year-old patient, "the importance of *not understanding* what she had not yet been able to give me clues for" (p. 222, Volume 11). Related to the restraint Winnicott describes throughout his writing is Stern's (1997) suggestion that an attempt toward neutrality lies inherently in the analyst's consistent and compassionate sense of curiosity. Winnicott is waiting for clues and curious to find them. For Winnicott (1968a), "waiting" was a crucial part of interpretation. He sees interpretation as a form of giving back to the patient because he has waited to find the patient's unwitting psychic foothold into their own unconscious process. I find this a useful ideal and one that includes many of our most significant contributions to understanding the activity of neutrality.

Clinical Vignette: R

R was 43 years old at the time of this vignette, four years into his analysis. He sought an analysis due to a nagging sense of anger toward his dominating and self-involved father. He struggled to shake his irritability toward his now-aging father's self-centeredness. R also felt especially impatient with male senior colleagues at his work, especially those whom he felt worked in undeservedly high positions. R was quite self-critical when his wishes to enjoy himself with his hobbies were in conflict with evening and weekend activities with his wife and two preschool-age daughters. Generally, he was actually quite available to his family, so we came to the conclusion that his wish to be different from his egocentric father was pressuring him, causing him to relentlessly criticize himself. He felt psychically drained by the concern that he was too much like his father.

R said that when he was a child, his father demanded that R's mother and sisters, one two years older and the other two years younger, revolve around his father's needs and interests. As R told it, his father was short-tempered and easily critical of R's mother and the kids, especially R's older sister. R felt guilty that he was not criticized as much as his older sister and felt that he had learned some ways to manipulate his father into leaving him alone. His sister was more prone to head-on collisions with R's father.

R and I did a great deal of work related to his anger at his father and his guilt about being less targeted than his older sister for his father's criticisms. He had felt cowardly about not standing up to his father more during his adolescence, despite the fact that he did express some of his anger. He was in a continual state of evaluating whether he was like his father, particularly when he asked his wife to subordinate her needs to his. R's wife would sometimes express anger at R when they had conflict, but her overall impression of R was that he was a devoted husband and father, not that he was only looking out for himself. So, despite their conflict at times about whose needs would take precedence, we came to see that R was burdened by the anxiety that he would be as selfish as his father rather than actually enacting this with his wife.

In a session four years into analysis, R began with the following dream. R is being held hostage by a group of men who are criminals. R is with a woman, and they are trying to save another woman who is missing but likely being held by the men. At some point, R and his female companion discover the missing woman, who is gagged and bound in a closet. They free her, but they realize that only one can get out to inform the authorities to come and help. R finds the police, but the detective in charge is skeptical of the story for a long time, wasting precious moments before the freed woman is discovered. Finally, he succeeds in convincing them of the need to come and arrest these men.

When I heard this dream, I was reminded of a dream R had told me about from childhood in which one of his parents' friends arrived to announce that he had killed R's father. The friend gave a somber rendering of the tale, but R was secretly pleased. R had the feeling that this man didn't want to kill the father but that "it had to be done."

The interpretations of the current dream that privately came to mind related to his familiar wish that he had done something to rescue or protect his sister. In the dream, he is insisting on the dangers of not doing so. The insensitivity and lack of concern by the police and the man in charge of helping are prominent. Silently, I wondered too if I was the detective in charge who was not understanding the danger for the woman being held. Had R felt that I was inadvertently minimizing how bad he had been to his sister by focusing on his self-criticism?

I did not mention this interpretation, both because it seemed accessible to R and because I was curious to see what came to his mind. He associated to wrestling games that he would play with his sisters, in which his older sister would pin him down or he would pin down his younger sister. He recalled the delight that he took in pinning his younger sister and that his older sister felt when pinning him. He then started talking about the point in his childhood when he could pin his older sister. He recalled how exciting it was for him to do this, and that when he learned he could pin her down, he began feigning that she was winning before pushing her over forcefully and pinning her.

R also associated to when he first realized at age 10 or 11 that pinning and being pinned by his older sister was sexually exciting. He was putting together some thoughts and feelings as he recalled the wrestling: how they both liked to emerge victorious, his enjoyment of the foolery and deceit toward his sister, and the physical sensations of their groin areas rubbing against each other.

Now I felt more inclined to speak of how R was the man who was earnestly seeking help for his sisters and mother, but at the same time, he too, not just his father, was represented in the figure who did not want to help. I told R that he was trying to understand parts of himself that were competitive, angry, and even excited about her captivity and his domination of her, all of which had been obscured by his guilt toward her. I said that in the dream, he was both a man seeking help for the captive girl and the man who was in some way indifferent. I then said that I thought he was trying to go further in the dream than he did when he simply attacked himself with his guilt.

R agreed and continued to associate. He said that he could actually feel that maybe he felt like the captive girl as well. He said that he had sometimes felt like one of the three girls (sisters and mother) since all four of them were in a different category of power than his father. I said to R that he had never told me about this feeling, to which R replied that he had never talked to anyone about it before, including his wife or friends.

There are many ways to describe these familiar practices that I include in activities related to neutrality. There is a necessary element of restraint in waiting and listening for R to come to his own associations to his dream. There is a kind of holding and respect that creates space for the patient to gather up "the bits and pieces" (Winnicott, 1968a) of his memories, thoughts, and feelings. I refer to these common practices here in the context of neutrality because I think of neutrality operating ubiquitously across many technical practices and precepts in analytic work.

In the subsequent hours as I reflected on R's dream, I began to think about elements of the transference and enactment in a slightly new way as well. R had never expressed anger or disappointment toward me during our analytic work. He was deeply appreciative of our work together. He was assertive about when he disagreed with something that I would say, and vocal about understanding all of my billing and vacation policies. Nevertheless, while he was not accommodating or passive, it did seem like R found me a bit unassailable.

I began to wonder whether I had failed to attend enough to the possibility that R avoided disagreement or conflict with me. Had I been minimizing his internal emergency about his feeling that he had not responded more actively to his father's aggression? Was I enacting the indifferent authority figure in the dream more than I'd already realized?

As I considered whether I was missing R's allusions to the transference prior to this dream and in his associations to the dream, I realized I felt that we were both aware of his potential experience of me as an indifferent detective and that I would have been only making an intellectualized interpretation of the dream. Instead, though, I wondered whether this line of inquiry led me to a position of concordance with R, namely that I worried I was at fault for something that was not my fault. R blamed himself even more than he had blamed either his father for his aggression and egocentricity, or his mother for her passivity and failure to protect her children. I was brought into a deeper emotional understanding of R's self-criticism, both through a better understanding of his excitement about his own sexual and aggressive feelings toward his sister, and through my own identification with a hyper-scrutinization of my analytic work.

In a sense, this form of self-reflection, which was an activity of neutrality, could be thought of as a new understanding of the transference-countertransference with R, a form of transference as the "total situation" (Joseph, 1985). We were each scrutinizing ourselves. My self-reflection was an activity of neutrality that led to elements of enacted identification with R (scrutinization that I hadn't done enough) that were different from those elements I was originally concerned about (whether he was angry at me for not doing more). Much of my thinking here was in the form of anterior and a posteriori thinking about the "total situation." Now the work with R turned to focus on the excitement and competitiveness with his sister that had promoted his self-reproach.

Concluding Remarks

One of the challenges posed by the complexity of neutrality in the analytic situation has always been related to the goal of psychoanalysis. The freedom to be oneself is the developmental ideal for most patients (e.g., Orgel, 2002). This ideal involves our radical surrender as analysts to a wish for our patient, in all of his similarity and otherness, to live. This ideal is perhaps translated by Arendt's (1996) definition of love as: "I want you to be" (Cooper, in press). The activity of neutrality is dedicated to this ideal, including, at its core, the wish for our patients to express as many of their feelings and thoughts as possible. As our vast literature charting the challenges of maintaining this position points out, the ideal of neutrality is linked to the process of trying – trying through our ongoing self-reflection, including our states of silent or verbalized anterior associations, restraint, immersion, the potential to be lost at times, and a posteriori understanding.

Examining our history of the use of the term "neutrality" leads us to question why the concept took on some of the surfeit meaning that it did. Was the more aseptic view of neutrality a necessary fantasy or construction to buttress the authority and credibility of the analyst in order to fend off skeptics or to increase the trust of patients? Or was it a necessary defense of sorts for the analyst to find an anchor rather than swim in the overwhelming complexity of the patient's unconscious mind and need to maintain balance? I suspect that all were true.

Despite the efforts of many to refine the meaning of the term "neutrality," and I include my own effort here, I find the term unsatisfying and lacking precision. I am reminded, though, of what Winnicott (1952) said about the term "depressive position." He found it highly problematic and unsatisfying but could think of no better term for what Klein had in mind for this bedrock concept. I have a similar feeling about the necessity of the term "neutrality" and have no better word to suggest as its replacement except to define it as a set of activities.

There is a somewhat vexing and humorous convergence of frustration with our attempts to put both the terms "neutrality" and "depressive position" into words. We must come to terms with the vagary of even our best attempts to articulate the meaning of "neutrality," which is elusive as both an activity and as an experience to name. Perhaps the vagary results from the way that the term contains a conceptual/semantic minimization of the complex, intersubjective core of the analytic process and the unconscious mind itself.

The concept of neutrality, then, as both a conceptual/semantic challenge and as a cluster of activities that are always in process and by definition always changing, is, in fact, an important part of the analyst's experience of the depressive position in analytic work. The activity of neutrality lays out a cluster of listening modes and ideals, at once never achievable but essential for the analyst to strive for and contain.

In the next chapter, I develop a more specific view of a particular function of neutrality as it is embedded in the nature of play, namely the way that play holds paradoxical realities during the analytic process.

References

Arendt, H. (1996) *Love and Saint Augustine,* ed. J. V. Scott and J. C. Stark. Chicago, IL: The University of Chicago Press.

Aron, L. (1991). The patient's experience of the analyst's subjectivity. *Psychoanalytic Dialogues* 1: 29–51.

Barthes, R. (1970) *S/Z*. New York: Hill & Wang.

Bion, W. (1970) *Attention and Interpretation.* London: Tavistock.

Bromberg, P. (1998) *Standing in the Spaces: Essays on Clinical Process, Trauma, and Dissociation.* London/Hinsdale, NJ: The Analytic Press.

Civitarese, G. (2008) *The Intimate Room: Theory and Technique of the Analytic Field.* London: New Library of Psychoanalysis.

Civitarese, G. (2013) Towards an ethics of responsibility. *Int. Forum of Psychoanal.* 20: 108–112.

Cooper, S. H. (1996) Neutrality and psychoanalysis: Separation, divorce, or a new set of vows? *J. Amer. Psychoanal. Assn.* 44: 1017–1019.

Cooper, S. H. (2016) *The Analyst's Experience of the Depressive Position: The Melancholic of Psychoanalysis.* London: Routledge.

Cooper, S. H. (2021) Toward an ethic of play. *Psychoanal. Q.* 90: 373–397.

Cooper, S. H. (2023) "I want you to be": Thinking about Winnicott's view of interpretation in ontological and epistemological psychoanalysis. In *Playing and Becoming in Psychoanalysis.* London/New York: Routledge.

Freud, A. (1936). *The Ego and the Mechanisms of Defence.* Abingdon, UK: Routledge, 2018.

Freud, S. (1914) Remembering, repeating, and working through. (Further recommendations on the technique of psychoanalysis). *SE* 12: 145–156.

Freud, S. (1954) *The Origins of Psycho-Analysis: Letters to Wilhelm Fliess, Drafts and Notes, 1887–1902,* ed. M. Bonaparte, A. Freud, and E. Kris. London: Imago, p. 486.

Greenberg, J. (1986) Theoretical models and the analyst's neutrality. *Contemp. Psychoanal.* 22: 87–106.

Hoffman, I. (1983) The patient as interpreter of the analyst's *Contemp. Psychoanal.* 19: 389–422.

Isaacs, S. (1948) The nature and function of phantasy. *Int. J. Psychoanal.* 29: 73–97.

Joseph, B. (1985) Transference: The total situation. *Int. J. Psychoanal.* 66: 447–454.

Kris, A. O. (1990) Helping patients by analyzing self-criticism. *J. Amer. Psychoanal. Assn.* 38: 605–636.

Mitchell, S. (2000) *Relationality*. Hillsdale, NJ: The Analytic Press.

Ogden, T. S. (1994) The concept of interpretive action. *Psychoanal Q.* 63: 219–245.

Ogden, T. S. (2024). Ontological analysis in clinical practice. *Psychoanal Q.* 2024: 93(1): 13–31.

Orgel, S. (2002) Some hazards to neutrality in the psychoanalysis of candidates. *Psychoanal Q.* 71(3): 419–443.

Renik, O. (1996) The perils of neutrality. *Psychoanal. Q.* 65: 495–517.

Steiner, J. (1994) Patient-centered and analyst-centered interpretations: Some implications of containment and countertransference. *Psychoanal. Inq.* 14(3): 406–422.

Stern, D. B. (1997) *Unformulated Experience: From Dissociation to Imagination in Psychoanalysis*. Hillsdale, NJ/London: The Analytic Press.

Wilson, M. (2013) Desire and responsibility: The ethics of countertransference experience. *Psychoanal. Q.* 82: 435–476.

Winnicott, D. W. (1952) The depressive position in normal emotional development. In *The Collected Works of D. W. Winnicott: Volume 4,* ed. L. Caldwell. Oxford: Oxford University Press, pp. 185–200.

Winnicott, D. W. (1968a) Interpretation in psychoanalysis. Originally published in *Psychoanalytic Explorations,* ed. C. Winnicott, R. Shepherd, and M. Davis. Cambridge, MA: Harvard University Press, 1989, pp. 207–212.

Winnicott, D. W. (1968b) Playing: A theoretical statement. In *Playing and Reality*. London: Tavistock, pp. 74–87.

Winnicott, D. W. (1977) *The Piggle: An Account of the Psycho-Analytic Treatment of Little Girl,* ed. I. Ramzey. London: Hogarth.

Wittgenstein, L. (1953) *Philosophical Investigations*. New York: MacMillan Publishing Company.

3 Playing, Paradox, and Analytic Activity between Knowing and Being

In a series of papers, I have tried to elaborate on how the holding of paradox that is carried out through play contributes to the therapeutic action of psychoanalysis. Here, I explore how this work has relevance to a consideration of the concept of neutrality in an ontologically informed psychoanalysis.

The analyst walks a line between not taking too much responsibility for the resolution of paradox while at the same time holding a frame for paradox to emerge and eventually to be better held by the patient. The analyst must trust that the analytic process will help the patient with holding paradox through the mourning of incompatible realities (e.g., Kris, 1985; Kristeva, 1992; Cooper, 2023).

Forms of resistance within the analyst occur when we feel pulled to remind the patient too quickly about the incompatibility of their wishes or when we get overly aligned with preserving the patient's wishes to hold both realities. Sometimes a cognitive understanding of the impossibility of the contrasting wishes will help the patient hold paradox. At other times, a cognitive understanding may interfere with the more natural elements of the patient's and analyst's play process, one that we hope will carry the patient into deeper experiences and often compassion toward holding these incompatible wishes.

Much of the analyst's effort to help the patient to hold paradox involves a posteriori activity of assessing these influences on the patient. I will examine how this element of posteriori activity carried out by the analyst at times overlaps with what I have referred to as an "activity of neutrality" (Cooper, 2022).

As we engage in play and make use of reverie, we are anything but neutral. Moreover, Wilson (2006, 2013) has suggested that intrinsic to the ethical context of psychoanalysis, it is necessary for the analyst to leave unadorned and protected both his lack and desire. Instead, the value of reverie is to heighten the analyst's capacity to connect with the patient in an associative way rather than be bound by the constraints of more secondary process-based thinking. The activity that I refer to as posteriori activity is a kind of abiding interest and assessment of the patient's capacity to hold paradox in play. This activity may involve engaging in continued listening, finding elements of further play, or offering more conventional interpretation that provide a cognitive scaffolding for holding experience. This activity and participation occur between

DOI: 10.4324/9781003569985-4

the spaces of the patient's and analyst's knowing and being in the analytic process.

Playing, Paradox, and Ontological Analysis

Psychoanalysis, as practiced in North America, Europe, and South America, has moved increasingly toward an emphasis on playing and dreaming as the theoretical undergirding for understanding psychoanalytic process. Or, at the very least, we have seen a movement toward integrating the ontological emphasis on playing and dreaming with the epistemological focus of Freud and Klein on knowing and understanding (e.g., Ogden, 2022).

I have been quite interested in playing as the theoretical undergirding for analytic process because Winnicott provided a way to describe the relationship between the actuality of objects and experience interacting with fantasy and potential space. As I have defined it (Cooper, 2018, 2021, 2023), playing in analysis with adults occurs through idiomatic expressions of unconscious fantasy, defense, and conflict expressed by patient or analyst in their lived experience together – what is verbally expressed, imagined, and experienced. The analyst often makes use of reverie that permits exploring elements of transference and intersubjective engagement and enactment. I have suggested that the rules of transference-countertransference engagement, that is, the way that patient and analyst are limited by the patient's unconscious conflicts and the analyst's, are temporarily loosened during playing (Cooper, 2021, in press).

While I view playing as the theoretical logic that undergirds all psychoanalytic process and that reverie is intrinsic to play, I try to not too sharply distinguish between ontological and epistemological threads in analytic work. These threads are always operating in concert with one another. For example, Aguayo's (2014) nuanced reading of Bion's notion of "without memory and desire" points to Bion's (1967) appreciation that there is an evolution of the analyst's memory that includes realistically necessary and often helpful retention of what has happened in prior sessions. From the beginning of ontological analysis, it is important to recall that both Winnicott and Bion had been so immersed in Kleinian thinking that the origins of ontological analysis already had many epistemological threads sewn in.

Moreover, each was developing methodologies that implicitly and explicitly recognized the actuality of the object in the person of the mother during development and the analyst in the clinical setting. The matter of the analyst's actuality as an object is important since Winnicott and Bion each understood in their distinctive ways that the psychoanalyst himself will become a threat to the analytic process. Their ways of describing guardianship of the setting addressed the limitations of the analyst that require continuous attention. The analyst's countertransference, responsive to the patient's wishes, fantasies, defenses, conflicts, or the analyst's wishes to cure the patient, provides both a portal as well as a source of resistance to helping the patient access unconscious experience. In my view, play often occurs in relation to the patient's and analyst's resistance to holding complex and conflictual experience.

As Winnicott and Bion brought psychoanalysis into an ontological realm without explicit elaboration of the topic of neutrality, they, de facto, shifted our focus from the content of interpretation to the various elements of the analyst's guardianship of the analytic setting. They elevated the holding and containing functions of our interpretive activities to equal standing with the interpretation of unconscious fantasy, transference, defense, and conflict. Playing and dreaming were necessary to provide an experience of psychic aliveness. They were also implying that it is primarily through guardianship that fresh insights can arrive for the patient rather than being issued by the analyst. For example, for Winnicott, playing itself was a therapy often more than the analysis of content of what playing revealed about unconscious experience.

For both Bion and Winnicott, a great deal of the guardianship of the setting was discovered in resisting obvious and available formulations (often already familiar to the patient) that were translated into interpretations. Winnicott (1968a) stated that he tried to interpret to show the patient the limits of his understanding. Patient and analyst are in the process of finding play, an activity in which patient and analyst move inside elements of illusion, inside elements of unconscious fantasy, defense, and transference-countertransference engagement (Cooper, 2021, 2023).

Bion's guardianship revolved around protecting the analyst's ability to process and contain what the patient struggled to contain (container-contained). In a sense, Bion was always trying to destabilize our familiar interpretive leanings, not so much to supplant them but to complement them to preserve a space to dream. Bion was suggesting that when we are leaning too heavily on overvalued ideas to find a receptive equilibrium (or the illusion of it), we are anything but neutral. The analyst as guardian of the setting involves a kind of holding of the fallibility of this container for the patient's and analyst's reverie.

There are obvious parallels between Winnicott's attempt to find play when the patient is unable to play and Bion's description of how the analyst lends his own capacity to process experience to the patient in the form of container-contained (e.g., Abram and Hinshelwood, 2023). Both Winnicott and Bion believed that we cannot expect to deal with unmentalized material exclusively by interpretation of content. Each aimed to go beyond conscious insight into unconscious conflicts. Each proceeded from Freud's (1914; 1925) insights in both "Remembering, Repeating and Working Through" and "A Note on the Mystic Writing Pad," that before we can verbalize unconscious phenomena and the transference, it is enacted and repeated. For both Winnicott and Bion, we cannot perform this function simply through thought. It requires an unusual degree of entry into the patient's experience and an unusual depth of reverie in the session. Meltzer (1986) referred to this activity as *counter-dreaming*.

I suggest that patients and analysts often operate quietly to establish a space between knowing and being in psychoanalytic work, one that may be obscured by theoretical explications that highlight one side or the other of the epistemological-ontological axis. Our patients' and our own wishes to know are an irrepressible part of analytic work, and importantly, they are also ways of being together. Our ways of being ourselves are also important ways of knowing ourselves and one another. In this way, the epistemological and ontological currents of analytic theory and technique are inextricably linked with one another. My guess is that approaches that favor the ontological or epistemological strand tend to emphasize more pure cultures of their approach rather than the hybridism in practice that characterizes most analytic work and is highly undertheorized.

Consider an analogy between the epistemological approach in psychoanalysis to music that has a classical form. The classical structure (e.g., note progression) creates in the listener an already certain sense of what will come next. We might say that the music creates an inevitable future. This was the kind of "music" that Bion cautioned against regarding our formulations. Yet we know that innovations in music, such as Beethoven's radical use of pauses and rests or Schoenberg's atonality, occur in relation to the classical form. The analyst's mind works productively in classical ways, and there is also much to be said for trying to open ourselves to what seems to come unbidden.

It is my impression that analysts are often instinctively moving between creating spaces for patients' and their own associations on the one hand, and observational forms of responsiveness on the other. For example, sometimes an analyst might feel that containment is served better by a form of responsiveness that emphasizes or frames something observed, such as in more conventional interpretation.

How Is the Holding of Paradox a Particular "Activity of Neutrality?"

Traditionally, the neutrality concept was applied to the ideal balance regarding the surface targeted in interpretation. For example, Anna Freud (1936) suggested that interpretations are ideally situated equidistant between elements of id, ego, and superego. Greenberg (1986) described a neutral stance as one in which the analyst is poised relatively equidistant between the patient's experience of the analyst as an old and new object.

These translations of the neutrality concept were each, in their own way, embedded within an epistemological approach to psychoanalytic work despite being aimed at different levels of theoretical discourse from each other. Anna Freud's interventions presuppose that the analyst can stand outside the patient's psyche to lend insight and knowledge about the patient's conflicts, defenses, and fantasies. While Greenberg's perspective considers that the analyst will inevitably be brought into the patient's experience and that there are reciprocally influencing processes, his view of neutrality is aimed at a different level of discourse than Winnicott's culture of playing as a lived experience between patient and analyst, one which valorizes the process of playing at least as much as the interpretations offered by the analyst.

In an earlier paper in which I developed a concept of the "activity of neutrality," I emphasized that more than ever, we appreciate both how many blind spots the analyst will have and the work required to make these blind spots usable. We also recognize that our assessments of neutrality are as likely to be suspect as anything else that we say or do in analytic work. Finally, a preoccupation with the ideal of neutrality runs the risk of disembodying analytic work, threatening to gloss over the jagged edges of analytic engagement. I offered a redefinition of neutrality from the point of view that we are always in various forms of transference-countertransference enactment (Cooper, 2022). We as analysts are always in relation to what the patient is expressing about their unconscious minds and feeling as well as to our own experiences and the psychoanalytic process itself (e.g., Parsons, 2006)

I suggested that neutrality is an activity on the part of the analyst, a verb rather than a noun. It is not a statically achievable state but instead an always-evolving process. The process of neutrality features, front and center, the analyst's thinking and curiosity about how to help a patient to know and become himself. It also features the analyst's process of posteriori self-reflection about inevitable enactment and where the analytic couple finds itself.

I add here that as guardians of the setting, we engage in specific activity related to preserving the analytic setting for the emergence of playing and the holding of paradox. Our guardianship of the setting is not intrinsically neutral. As analysts, we are trying to open ourselves "to the instruments inside us" (Whitman, 1855), which requires a vast range of experiences and fantasy. The music can be loud, soft, fast, slow, melodic, or unmelodious. The element of holding paradox that relates to an activity of neutrality resides in the varieties of ways that we make use of these experiences.

Specifically, I suggest that an activity of neutrality involves elements of the analyst's subtle contemporaneous and posteriori efforts to help the patient to hold paradox rather than prematurely truncate a process of play. At times, the analyst works to avoid more cognitively oriented forms of responsiveness that seek a kind of pressured, pseudo-resolution between mutually incompatible wishes and fantasies. Sometimes this activity is no more than listening in order to honor the patient's ongoing attempts to hold paradox through play. The other side of this listening involves the analyst's readiness to provide a cognitive scaffolding for experiences that are overwhelming regarding holding mutually incompatible wishes. At these times, the analyst frames the content of what the patient is struggling to hold regarding seemingly opposite or mutually exclusive wishes and fantasies.

The analytic setting itself also holds the strange paradox that psychoanalysis is a space that is, *in private in public*. I think of this strange paradox as a way of considering reverie and playing as two currents in the analytic process in which our private reveries, those of the patient and analyst, are selectively brought into usage. Play exposes, accentuates, often performs, and holds paradox. Playing makes use of our reverie (reverie is an object here that is being used) from time to time, or, put another way, we arrive at playing as we try to make use of our associations. In play, reverie is an emergent experience that itself takes on the status of an object and is played with and becomes useful through processes of play and destruction/usage.

I will try to illustrate through an extended vignette how play operates in relation to the holding of paradox and how some particular activities of the patient and analyst help to sustain that holding.

Clinical Vignette

C

C is a married man in his early 50s with considerable leadership responsibilities in the business he founded. By all accounts, he has been quite successful as an entrepreneur, but he often feels that he withdraws from confrontation with his employees. He began undergoing analysis three times a week to understand his wishes to withdraw from challenging instances when he needs to assert his authority as a leader, both at the level of inspiring the 40 people who work for him as well as having to meet with employees and help them improve or fire them.

C describes his parents as each "big distinctive personalities" who demanded that he and his two older sisters accommodate their needs, especially his mother's needs. His mother could be very lively and vivacious, but her moods were volatile. In a way that seemed unpredictable, she would abruptly become angry and then turn to a dark, depressive, and withdrawn mode. His father seemed to be somewhat impervious to the mother's fluctuations in moods but also oblivious to how C would dread his mother's depressive and angry moods. C's two older sisters were thoughtful toward C about his sensitivity and anxiety, but he only felt a modicum of comfort from them despite their efforts. Whether it was his fantasy or true, his sisters seemed tougher to him and less influenced by his mother's moods.

C alternated between defiance and accommodation. He felt that though he could try to talk back to his parents or defy them, he suffered from anxiety. He linked his anxiety with his parents about expressing himself to his reluctance to confront employees and colleagues despite his position of authority in relation to them. C quaked when he had to fire employees or even do what he thought necessary as the leader of his company.

The session that I summarize from a period about one year into his analysis follows from several sessions in recent weeks in which we'd been examining something that he had said to his parents when he was around seven years old. C is shocked that he told his parents around age seven, at one point when his mother was "withdrawn and sulking" and asking him to leave her alone, "I don't love you anymore and I will have to leave." When he brought this up in analysis for the first time, he began laughing, and I did as well. We were stunned by the dramatic effect and power of his words to his parents and how at odds it was with his current anxiety about confrontation with others. It is also at odds with how much he had described himself so far in the analysis as having been frightened and anxious about his mother's temper.

C's father is deceased, but C remains quite anxious when interacting with his mother when she is unhappy about something he has done regarding visits and impending decisions that he and his sisters will have to make with her regarding her long-term care.

Session

C: I'm struggling to finish up a speech that I must give to the company. I think that I'm saying some things that are necessary but that I know in advance will make some people angry or want to push back at me. I get these talks to a certain point in my writing and then I have two people I really trust who edit it and give me feedback. They work for me but somehow, I feel intimidated by them.

Analyst (I am thinking to myself about whether he is editing himself here or concerned about my feedback about what he is saying but I remain quiet and listen to him. Am I in the group he trusts, or not, or both?).

C: Lately as I think about this speech and having to finish it up and give it to my colleagues for their feedback, I have this strong feeling of wanting to take a nap.

I don't know how to make sense of myself as this little boy who was so dramatic and had such flair to say what I said to my parents and this anxious guy now. I had almost completely forgotten that I ever said that to my parents until we started talking about it. And I did actually forget it until one day my middle sister was laughing about it one night when we had a lot to drink. She thought it was the funniest thing she'd ever heard.

I don't know whether I ever told you this, but I used to look through magazines when I was a boy and I would try to decide who my real parents were. It was as if I was inventing them. I guess I did it when I wasn't happy about something that they did or said. I think that I was especially trying to invent who my mother was. Her moods just really got to me. They took over everything in the family. My father would lose his temper when he was in a bad mood, but otherwise he didn't take over things. My mom was just always demanding that everything be about her. (Long Pause)

I'm thinking about something that my therapist said to me when I was in therapy in my early twenties. We had a session around Mother's Day, and he said, "Do you know what the busiest day is at the baths in San

Francisco and New York? Mother's Day." I don't know whether my therapist was gay. I know that he was married. Maybe I wondered if he was gay. Or, I'm not sure how much I wondered about it then, but I seem to be wondering about it now.

(I am listening, wondering if he is feeling that as we get deeper into what made him say these things to his parents and is telling me more about his vulnerability with them and his employees if he is frightened by our closeness. I'm also wondering if he is feeling a need for me as a father to help him with his mother, whom he feels dominated by.) Is he feeling the closeness as something in him that makes him feel "gay" or that I am gay or that we are gay together?

Analyst: I think that you want to feel free to speak with the authority that you have but at the same time avoid your mother's anger because you feel that she can't tolerate you being who you are. You could only threaten to leave or fantasize about getting new parents rather than feel shut down.

C: I do want them to want me to be myself and they didn't like it when I felt I was being most myself. I didn't enjoy the activities that they enjoyed but I was seen as recalcitrant and difficult.

Analyst: This is when you said "I won't be able to love you anymore. I'll have to leave."

C: Yes, I think it was when they didn't like me saying what I felt.

Analyst: The vitality that you have found in your work or the demands of having to set limits with those who work for you is always being threatened with the memories of someone telling you not to be who you are or asking you to be organized around them.

C: I'm thinking of seeing my mother for Mother's Day. It must be why I was having that memory of my former therapist telling me that about Mother's Day. We will go out for brunch with one of my sisters who lives here and my mother will have a drink and get tipsy and only want to talk about old times. I don't like it. I dread it. I feel like I'm getting sucked into something that I don't want to get into. I know that I'll be ok when I see her, but I don't have good memories of those times.

Analyst: You don't know if you can know what you do know. You know that you couldn't invent new parents. You know that your mother will have her drink and you will feel the pull to give up on yourself and take a nap. Or to deny who they are and find some new parents. And I think that you are wondering if you can allow yourself to want to know me and for me know you, or will you have to invent me.

C: Well, I do want to know you, but I wasn't wondering whether you were gay if that's where you are getting some of this from. I haven't thought that you were gay, but I suppose that you could be.

Analyst: I was thinking that your former therapist was discussing the baths as a place for men to console, comfort, and excite themselves with the complexity of their mother feelings.

C: I was thinking that too. I just don't know what to do with the part of me that wants to take a nap and give up. I guess I fight through it but I wish that I didn't have to fight it. (Long pause) My mother, for as long as I've known her has been the way she is.

(I, {analyst}, am a bit stunned by this turn of phrase here and he is quiet for what seems like a long time but is likely no more than 30 seconds).

C: Wow, I can't believe I just said that! My mother for as long as I've known her. For as long as I've known her. (He begins laughing here and is incredulous about what he's said as am I).

(Again, there is a long pause. This was a comment that in my mind was bordering on a parapraxis. I began a long set of associations to the idea that it sounded like C was God. I began thinking about the leading character in the play *Sisyphus* [Critias, fragment in Camus, 1955], who promoted the idea that a very shrewd and subtle man invented the fear of gods to frighten other men from acting in ways that were wicked. I was thinking that C, in his unconscious fantasy, was God or that as a boy he'd wanted to create a God that would make his wicked parents behave as he wished. C, a faithless boy, was hoping for a solution. I must have also been thinking about *Sisyphus* in connection with the eternal futility that C engaged in by a fantasy about new parents rather than mourning the ones he'd had.)

Analyst: It sounds like you were around before she was! That you were around for a period of time before you knew her, maybe the way a parent is around before the birth of his or her child.

C: Yes!

Analyst: You felt in some ways like you were a parent to her, but it's also got that same quality of inventing her and yourself in relation to her. Here before your mother.

C: I guess I'm doing the same thing aren't I? I'm pretending that she's not my mother.

Analyst: But it catches up with you when you want to execute your own, real authority. You still hold on to wanting someone to know and be interested in what you think. Maybe you don't even want to have to say it.

(I'm thinking that for C, separation from them has meant trying to reinvent them, which is in fact a way to not separate.)

C: It's so strange because my working small group wants to know what I have to say, and they also know that they are required to want to know what I have to say whether they like it or not because I am their boss. But I actually think that they value what I have to say.

Analyst: I don't think that you are especially concerned about your employees. You are attached to your parents wanting to hear you and can't entirely give them up. And you can't reinvent them. They were and are your parents just like I am your analyst.

C: You mean my analyst for as long as I have known him?

We each smiled here as the session needed to end, albeit in a density of feeling that I will try to deconstruct a bit here.

Discussion of Session

This is a relatively simple example of how C is moving into protean versions of play in relation to his experience. By simple, I mean that C is the one to bring us to the point of play, and I tried to meet him there. It also illustrates how, through our provision of the setting and our responsiveness through listening and interpretation, psychoanalysis works toward the holding of incompatible realities.

C brings us deeply into the way he was looking to create his own parents with his own rules. He isn't just talking *about* it. Through his idiomatic language (e.g., "my mother for as long as I have known her"), C is also bringing us into the moment when he escapes into fantasy. C also brings me into the mix in the transference by saying, with his mix of humor and the psychic effort involved in denial, "My analyst, for as long as I have known him." It is important that when C brings us into the transference in his playful comment about me, he does so after I have offered a more conventional interpretation about his employees being stand-ins for his wishes for his parents to have more interest in him. He is moving into play from my efforts to understand. This is what I mean by the way that patient and analyst move quietly between epistemological and ontological elements of analytic work.

C's language also illustrates what I refer to as entering further inside the rules of transference-countertransference engagement. C feels that his only way to overcome his mother is to deny that she is his mother. His words suggest that C met her acquaintance in ways that he has met others and that I am his analyst for as long as he has known me. One of the most interesting characteristics of this language is that it is all grammatically correct, unassailable from that point of view. Yet it is an unusual turn of phrase to direct toward a parent.

First, there is a potentially meaningful caesura (Bion, 1974a; Civitarese, 2008a) after he realizes what he has said about his mother. He pauses because he is struck with an obvious breakthrough of an unconscious fantasy. In this moment, C may be bearing something, becoming aware of something in his idiomatic language that is overwhelming in its scope. He is experiencing himself in the moment of defense and unconscious fantasy, in which he is trying to create his mother as he wishes.

His play, as is often the case, is so meaningful because it demonstrates something being acted out, staged from within unconscious experience. He leads by bringing me into his verbal, idiomatic construction, trying to hold a paradoxical reality between me in "diachronic time and synchronic time" (e.g., Ogden, in press). In diachronic time, he is telling me a version of what happened to him in the past with his mother, but he is bringing it into synchronic time in the analysis by experiencing and saying, "my analyst, for as long as I have known him." It is not yet clear what he means by this statement about me. Does he expect me to hurt him too? Does he have to invent a new analyst to mitigate anxiety about not being seen? Is he already feeling closer to me and anxious about this experience, already living inside those experiences with me now? At this moment, I was unable to speak to which, or all of these might be operating.

The analyst is the guardian of these temporary states of ambiguity and paradoxicality that correspond to matters of what is being contained and by whom (Cooper, 2000; Civitarese, 2008a, 2008b). My stance moves back and forth between highlighting the pull of incompatible wishes through verbal, secondary process scaffolding on one side, and, on the other, simply listening to the ambiguity about the elements that C is trying to metabolize. There is ambiguity about in what ways these elements are also protean expressions of play. And there is ambiguity about whether our attempts to integrate what we are hearing are in fact further forms of enactment of the transference. If symbolization is in a state of continuous tension with its own undoing (Civaterese, 2008a), it is sometimes very difficult to determine the difference between beta-elements and other thoughts. The analyst's ability to hold this ambiguity and to tolerate frustration is of course a major part of his or her guardianship of the setting.

My activity here involves minimal verbal interpretation, instead honoring C's considerable efforts to hold the paradoxical realities of his wishes to be attached to his parents while inventing them as he wishes them to be. My efforts are directed toward a reminder of reality only toward the end of the session when I affirm to him that his parents and his analyst exist, outside his attempts to reinvent his parents through omnipotent fantasy. I remind him of this only after he has done the work of moving in and out of the holding of impossibility of incompatible realities. This element of restraint and listening to the patient's efforts to hold paradox is an example of an activity of neutrality aimed at not interfering with the patient's process of arriving at new experiences of self (e.g., Winnicott, 1968a, 1968b). C is in a process of taking on how, in inventing his parents, he is acting as they did by getting to know him less as he was and more dictating to him whom they wished him to be. He also wishes to know and not know about his homoerotic feelings toward men and me. Most importantly, he wishes to separate from his parents but not mourn them!

More About the Work with C

C had to contend with the instability of holding these incompatible affective pulls. Two months after this session, C began missing more appointments due to work conflicts. I charge my patients when they miss for work unless we can reschedule a makeup session (usually quite realistic) or if I can fill the hour with another meeting. C began protesting this policy, even though we had been working this way for a year and a half. Stating that his work was requiring him now to miss more sessions, C said that making up the sessions would be difficult, even though he understood why I have this policy for myself and how it could work for other patients but was challenging for him. I was sympathetic to him but felt that what he was experiencing was complex.

I thought that C was likely engaging in a version of play, more deeply exploring and enacting his places of conflict and unconscious fantasy. Here, he is trying to create his own framework in which he can invent our rules of engagement and speak up about his wishes. Yet his wishes to do so, his own new rules, conflict with those of mine that dictate my practice and how I think about work. He is engaging in another version of looking in a magazine for a new analyst/parent, but he is also doing something different with his sadness and anger, lobbying for me to see and accommodate his needs.

C and I tried to tease this apart. C was in many ways going back and forth between what seemed like a genuine understanding of my policies regarding missed sessions and finding them, in his words, "unworkable." At one point, as we were examining his wish to create his own setting, his own analyst, and his own parents as enacted with me, I said to him, "Your analyst, for as long as you have known him has had this policy." He laughed about this and paused. He said, "I am seeing what you're doing here. You're saying that we are in something together about this." I agreed, and he returned to the same position of insisting that he was right and that it didn't matter whether it was always my policy.

My interpretive effort here was to bring in the reality of my consistent setting, one that he had always known about, to frame and hold his anger and frustration that my existence felt like indifference toward him. We continued working on this matter in relation to our setting for many sessions while we tried to reschedule, and he paid me for my time under protest. These misses were quite infrequent despite his statement that he would need to miss often. C was able to experience how much more deeply he wanted me and his parents to see him as a unique boy, not someone incorporated into his family.

Among the many interesting things that occurred during these sessions was C's growing awareness that he could often reschedule make-up sessions but was withholding some aspects of his scheduling flexibility. He realized that his reluctance to do so was related to wanting to hold on to his grievance and not feel that he was submitting to my rules and theirs.

I commented on how much he had entered a new institutionalized set of rules in our analytic family with me and that he was trying to see if something different could happen. C was able eventually to see how much he was performing in some sense and experiencing an ability to protest and speak about his desires while having me be interested in what he was saying in ways that he had not been previously able to do.

Through the lens of playing in psychoanalytic work, C is attempting to mourn and not mourn his sense of not being seen by his parents. In inventing parents, acting like the boy who could withhold his love and have all that power, he was beginning to understand that he didn't get to be the actual disappointed boy who wanted to be better recognized. Nor did it permit an actual feeling of empowerment (despite being quite effective in the real world) that comes through the survival of disappointment with reality. As an analyst, I am trying to protect a place for acknowledging his fraught and ambivalent efforts to hold a paradoxical reality about his wishes to be seen; a reality that his parents were who they were; and that I am who I am with my rules of engagement.

In the density of transference, he is trying to make use of me as an analyst, while at the same time also trying to invent me and us as he wishes us to be, "for as long as he has known me." The rules that apply to him and applied to him were not fair, and, like in all play, he is trying to reinvent rules. We are enacting a repetition of an original failure while our own analytic awareness of paradox informs how we are trying to facilitate the emergence of new experience.

It is important to note that here I see C's attack on the setting as occurring in the context of a repetition of earlier feelings of having to accommodate in his family. I view his aggression partly in line with Winnicott's (1969) notion of positive or creative aggression since he is exerting psychic effort toward holding paradoxical realities. This stands in contrast to a view of his aggression as more exclusively seeking revenge and grievance, both of which were indeed also in operation here.

Analysts hold a setting for these paradoxical realities, allowing ourselves to become part of a "process of restoring the paradoxical space of thirdness that holds the old and the new" (Benjamin, 2016, p. 587). Both play and paradox are the underlying, perhaps obvious but unseen, undergirding of what allows us to make use of transference. There is a quality to what C and I are doing here in which we are performing something about what happened to him earlier with his parents while he is also experiencing it now with me.

When I said to C, "Your analyst, for as long as you have known him has had this policy," I am speaking from inside our play and framing this in a few ways worth examining. First, C says to me, "I see what you are doing here. You're saying that we are in something together." We are both making more explicit our framework for working on this together, a framework which has been operating well despite his frustration and anger about it. When I made this comment, I believe that I was doing so without getting "ahead of the patient's transference confidence" (Winnicott, 1968b, p. 311). Winnicott's statement was the closest that he came to discussing neutrality. He was describing how problematic it can be when transference interpretations are offered without patients being ready to genuinely link the observation to a lived experience. My comment recognized C's deep and experientially alive similarity between his experience of his parents and me in our work together.

C is also responding to my comment by executing some framing of his own here for holding paradox. When he says that he sees what I am doing, my experience was not that he was primarily suspicious of my comment. Instead, he introduces the words to acknowledge that he feels simultaneously my attempt to help him both be in this experience with me trying to help and to understand something about his more fraught experiences of being told to acclimate to another. C is taking responsibility for the shared elements of our work together, and I read his process of taking responsibility for what is happening as a signal that providing additional secondary process understanding will help to hold an experience of aliveness rather than create distance from it.

With regard to the axes of knowing and being, my remark is both inside our play but also helping him to know and see more (with me) regarding what we are doing together. It is an example of how interpretations are often an implicit activity that operates to hold tension between knowing and experiencing/being. I underscore that here we are often quietly taking measure of the balance between the patient's experiences inside the transference and the need to hold it or frame it in a verbalized understanding. We engage in this activity in the moment and, of course, as we listen to the patient's associations over time.

Concluding Remarks

A thread running throughout this chapter is that many analysts, regardless of theoretical perspective, may be operating back and forth between facilitating our patients' experiences of knowing and being. Psychoanalysis is obviously predicated on the notion that without being in an experience, we can't come to understand something about it. It has been well established that Winnicott and Bion's theoretical and technical writing were redressing a problem in clinical analysis in which, in their view, knowing had often remained at too much remove from living an experience.

My description of a particular activity of neutrality as it relates to the analyst's interpretive efforts and restraint in helping patients to hold incompatible realities and paradox operated implicitly in some of the writing of Loewald (1960) and Kris (1985). Loewald's descriptions of the subtle density in interpretations that meet a patient where they are and challenge them to examine something new in anticipating their growth aimed to help patients to hold paradox. Loewald described that good interpretations hold this balance for respecting the patient's current stability while imagining their future psychic growth. Through an ego psychological lens and without reference to paradox, A. Kris (1985) beautifully described a mourning process related to holding incompatible wishes in divergent conflict. While I prefer to see these shifts through the lens of playing, there is overlap between Kris's (1985) focus on the mourning of incompatible wishes and my own through a mourning process in play (Cooper, 2023), one that cultivates similar emergent capacities of patients to be able to hold these forms of paradox in new and enriching ways.

As developed in this paper, the epistemological and ontological dimensions of analytic work are often linked with one another in the analyst's attempts to facilitate the holding of paradox in play. My work with C underscored the analyst's generally routine attempts to honor the patient's own ability to hold paradox. This requires restraint at times from more cognitively oriented efforts to acknowledge the incompatible realities that the patient is already trying to hold in stops and starts through play. At other times, it requires a framing of what the patient is struggling to do to support the cracks in these efforts.

The obvious problem with a too exaggerated search for knowing and understanding is that it can sometimes take us away from helping a patient discover that playing may be its own therapy in analysis. For example, when C was protesting my fee arrangements, I was tempted to explain to him more than I did that he might be unconsciously trying to make sure that I knew what it felt like to live with a set of rules that are unfair and that don't feel oriented to him as a person (e.g., projective identification). I am quite certain that he already knew this might be operating and that I thought so. Eventually, we were able to speak of this together from places inside a more lived experience in his transference experience of me as having rules that, in effect, marked a kind of indifference to his needs. As I have suggested here, the analyst's assessment of these processes is a part of the activity of neutrality.

Here, I simply explained to him why I have the policy that I do because C could hold his sense of my impinging on him and disappointing him. Obviously, for some patients who might be more overwhelmed by a negative transference experience related to the frame or trauma, the analyst needs to provide a more ongoing cognitive framing structure to help the patient metabolize their experience (e.g., Benjamin, 2016).

Through a series of papers, Winnicott (1945, 1968a, 1968b) described the analytic situation as a "place" for the patient to live an experience in which creative parts of the patient are voiced and discovered. He suggested that the holding of paradox is intrinsic to being alive and creative, including all the desires and prohibitions that mediate our experience of being alive. The premature or pseudo-resolution of paradox leads to increasing emphasis on defensive organization. The essence of the guardianship of the setting is that it is the analyst who needs to ensure that what goes on in the work is seen as existing inside a framework for understanding that transference is both real and unreal at the same time.

We have many limitations in speaking of what we mean by experience coming alive (Ogden, 2022, in press). I think that both C and I felt that he was coming alive in the material that I've presented here. Since play often involves an ongoing possibility of the rules of play changing, there are challenges involved in determining the precarious nature of coming alive in the context of safety and stability. The important matter is less whether one analyst would make a different decision than another, and more that the analyst feels that he or she is able to protect the symbolic realm as a place to make meaning of the patient's and analyst's feelings and thoughts. The analytic setting holds a unique intersubjective history in which we protect a frame through our self-reflective activity for holding these experiences in the present, just as we often anticipate a patient's potential growth in the future.

References

Abram, J. and Hinshelwood, R. D. (2023) *The Clinical Paradigms of Donald Winnicott and Wilfred Bion*. New York: Routledge.

Aguayo, J. (2014) Bion's notes on memory and desire – Its initial clinical reception in the United States: A note on archival material. *Int. J. Psycho-Anal.* 95: 889–910.

Benjamin, J. (2016) From enactment to play: Metacommunication, acknowledgement, and the third of paradox. *Rivista Di Psicoanalisi.* 62: 565–593.

Bion, W. R. (1967) Notes on memory and desire. *Psychoanal. Forum* 2: 272–280.

Bion, W. R. (1974) Bion's Brazilian lectures 1 — São Paulo. In *Brazilian Lectures*. Revised and corrected edn. London: Karnac, 1990.

Camus, A. (1955) *The Myth of Sisyphus*. New York: Alfred A. Knopf.

Civitarese, G. (2008a) 'Caesura' as Bion's discourse on method. *Int. J. Psycho-Anal.* 89: 1123–1143.

Civitarese, G. (2008b) Immersion versus interactivity and analytic field. *Int. J. Psycho-Anal.* 89: 279–298.

Cooper, S. H. (2000) Mutual containment in the analytic situation. *Psychoanal. Dial.* 10: 169–194.

Cooper, S. H. (2018) Playing in the darkness: Use of the object and use of the subject. *J. Amer. Psychoanal. Assn.* 66(4): 743–765.

Cooper, S. H. (2021) Toward an ethic of play. *The Psychoanal. Quar.* 90: 373–397.

Cooper, S. H. (2022) The activity of neutrality. *The Psychoanal. Quar.* 91: 355–369.

Cooper, S. H. (2023) The play of mourning. *J. Amer. Psychoanal. Assn.* 71: 61–82.

Cooper, S. H. (2024) The virtual Oedipal citadel: Varieties of isolation, Oedipal conflict, and cover-up. *J. Amer. Psychoanal. Assn.* 72: 613–635.

Freud, A. (1936) *The Ego and the Mechanisms of Defense*. London: Hogarth Press.

Freud, S. (2014) Remembering, repeating and working through (Further recommendations on psychoanalytic technique). *SE* 12: 144–156.

Freud, S. (1925) A note upon the "Mystic Writing-Pad" (Standard Edition, Vol. 19). London: Hogarth, p. 230.

Greenberg, J. (1986) The problem of analytic neutrality. *Contemporary Psychoanalysis* 22: 76–86.

Kris, A. O. (1985) Resistance in convergent and divergent conflicts. *Psychoanal. Q.* 54: 537–568.

Kristeva, J. (1992) *Black Sun*. New York: Columbia University Press.

Loewald, H. (1960) On the therapeutic action of psychoanalysis. *Int. J. Psychoanal.* 41: 16–33.

Meltzer, D. (1986) II. What is an emotional experience? In *Studies in Extended Metapsychology: Clinical applications of Bion's ideas,* ed. D. Meltzer. London: Harris Meltzer Trust, 143: 21–33.

Ogden, T. (2022) *Coming to Life in the Consulting Room: Toward a New Analytic Sensibility*. London: Routledge.

Ogden, T. (2024) Rethinking the concepts of the unconscious and analytic time. *Int. J. Psychoanal.* 105(3): 279–291.

Parsons, M. (2006) The analyst's countertransference to the analytic process. *Int. J. Psychoanal.* 87: 1183–1198.

Wilson, M. (2006) "Nothing could be further from the truth": The role of lack in the analytic process. *Journal of the American Psychoanalytic Association* 54: 397–421.

Wilson, M. (2013) Desire and responsibility: The ethics of countertransference experience. *Psychoanalytic Quarterly* 82: 435–476.
Whitman, W. (1855) *Leaves of Grass*. New York: Dover Press.
Winnicott, D. W. (1945) Primitive emotional development. In *Through Paediatrics to Psychoanalysis*, ed. D. W. Winnicott. New York: Basic Books, 1958, pp. 145–156.
Winnicott, D. W. (1967) Winnicott's letter to Bion. In *The Collected Works of D. W. Winnicott: Volume 8*, ed. L. Caldwell and H. T. Robinson. Oxford: Oxford Academic, pp. 201–220.
Winnicott, D. W. (1968a) Interpretation in psycho-analysis. In *The Collected Works of D. W. Winnicott: Volume 8, 1967*, ed. L. Caldwell, and H. T. Robinson. Oxford: Oxford Academic, pp. 253–258.
Winnicott, D. W. (1968b) The place where we live. In *The Collected Works of D. W. Winnicott*, ed. L. Caldwell and H. T. Robinson. Oxford: Oxford Academic, pp. 221–227.
Winnicott, D. W. (1969) The use of the object. *Int. J. Psycho-Anal.* 50: 711–716.

4 Winnicott's Paradox of Being with and without Memory and Desire

Notes on a Letter from Winnicott to Bion

I will use Winnicott's (1967) letter, written to Bion after his lecture on negative capability, to reflect on what I regard as a most intriguing historical moment in post-Freudian psychoanalytic theory and practice. I focus on a personal reading about several theoretical issues that might have been at play as Winnicott raised questions about Bion's lecture.

Winnicott's letter to Bion stimulates a few questions about important areas of overlap and difference between the two theorists. If anything, I'm surprised that Winnicott's objections to the paper were not stronger, raising the question of whether he was writing a courteous, collegial letter that belied some significant objections. It is possible that Winnicott was actually referring as much to Bion's paper, "Notes on Memory and Desire" (Bion, 1967, 1970), than the lecture on negative capability which immediately preceded the letter.

My reading of Winnicott's letter to Bion leads me to an assemblage of foci in Winnicott's writing about maternal preoccupation, being the guardian of play and the analytic setting, surviving the infant's and patient's destruction, and being both an actual and symbolic object in the analytic process. Each of these areas involves the analyst and mother holding a particular position of being with and without desire in their actions. To wit, the capacity to hold paradox is at the center of Winnicott's writings about interpretive stance, one that he felt promoted individuals' ability to live a creative life (Winnicott, 1968a, 1968b, 1968c).

To state my thesis as succinctly as possible, albeit a speculative one, Winnicott's differences with Bion's statement that the analyst should be without memory and desire revolve around Winnicott holding on to various forms of paradox. I believe that his position requires the analyst to strive toward holding that he or she will be both with and without memory and desire. I will address how his views on the areas of maternal preoccupation, playing, temporality, and what I will call creative aggression contributed to Winnicott's reflections on Bion's suggestion to listen without memory and desire.

One notion that informs my thinking about Winnicott's letter to Bion is the belief that throughout his writing, Winnicott is deeply interested in both the actuality and symbolic value of the object as they contribute to development and the therapeutic action of psychoanalysis. In the transitional object

DOI: 10.4324/9781003569985-5

paper, he underscores the value of the transitional object as related to it being an actual object, not simply symbolic. He emphasizes in "The Use of the Object" that the subject destroys the object "because the object is placed outside the area of omnipotent control" but also that it is the destruction of the object "that places the object outside the area of omnipotent control" (Winnicott, 1969, p. 90). I have argued (e.g., 2018) in agreement with many other authors (e.g., Bromberg, 1998; Ogden, 2016; Bonaminio, 2012) that the patient's experience of the analyst's actuality, such as the fear of being destroyed, is a part of the movement from relating to usage. I believe that the kind of actual object that Winnicott described is a different kind of actual object than the one Bion described.

Similarly, in his two major papers on play (Winnicott, 1968a, 1968b), Winnicott is not especially concerned with who initiates play. For example, in his theoretical paper about play, the analyst became a wellspring of motivation for play (Winnicott, 1968a). Winnicott is more interested in whether play or any form of interpretation is getting ahead of the patient's ability to integrate what is occurring between patient and analyst, what he referred to as the patient's transference confidence, than whether the analyst's motivations initiate play.

The Letter

I will quote only the first part of the letter, which is the part related to Bion's lecture and the focus of my paper:

> Dear Bion,
>
> First, to thank you for a very interesting evening.
>
> I am not quite settled in my mind about the idea of memory and desire or intention. When I got home, Clare reminded me again that the phrase memory and desire, which you have used before, is a quotation from T. S. Eliot, and she was able to give me the whole poem, and for some reason or other I accept memory and desire as naturally interrelated in the poem. At the same time, in the application of the same idea to psycho-analytic work I cannot help finding myself using the word intention and not feeling desire to be correct. As you said, we each have to find the word that fits for oneself. For me, memory and desire is all right in a poem because it refers to an experience that is 100% subjective. In the application of psycho-analytic work I find I cannot allow that this is 100% subjective. The memory includes memories of phenomena from external reality and certainly what is likely to turn up tomorrow in my analytic work cannot be covered by what I have in my own mind to want, precisely because I have to be able to allow the patient to be a separate person, as the patient has to come to be able to allow me to be outside his or her omnipotent control.
>
> So you see why is that I find myself unhappy with your word desire in this context.

As you can see, Winnicott found the concept of "without memory and desire" quite intriguing but preferred the word "intention" over "desire" because analytic work is not purely subjective in the way that poetry is. For Winnicott, the notion of the analyst's intentions was more applicable to the ways he wished to work with his memories of phenomena from external reality that he had already formed, "because I have to be able to allow the patient to be a separate person, as the patient has to come to be able to allow me to be outside his or her omnipotent control" (p. 158).

Let's address the implications of desire versus intention along several different dimensions.

The Actuality of the Object and the Paradox of Being with and without Desire

Winnicott's response to Bion captures the ethic of working with our intentions in order to use, construct, and destroy our affective and cognitive sketches along the way in knowing our patients and ourselves with our patients. It is an arduous process, one that Bion elaborated on perhaps more than any other analyst. Winnicott ends his note to Bion, reminding him that Bion himself had stated in this and many other writings that it is important for each of us each to find our own ways of referring to this process, including our own language.

Winnicott's primary objection to the words "without memory and desire" involves the fact that as an actual person and analyst, Winnicott knows that he has many desires and memories. He cannot be without them through fiat.

Part of the analyst's experience of the analytic process and of himself involves a kind of unlearning, or maybe we could even say parricide, toward elements of the analytic process with each patient. If we think of working as a psychoanalyst as always involving a tension between applying a body of learned technique (received wisdom) and our own individual sensibilities applied to the unique person with whom we are working, there is always a process of destruction that is occurring.

Winnicott's notion of the actuality of the object suggests that he is describing himself in the analytic process as real to himself and to some extent the patient. He is not wanting to push away too much of what makes him real, such as memory and desire. Having said that, I imagine that Winnicott must have been aware of Bion's interest in the analyst's own disturbed attention in listening.

Both Winnicott and Bion were, in their own revolutionary ways, working with the actuality of the object (mother and analyst) in ways that were at odds with their Kleinian training. They were each struggling with this fact both in their theory development and likely in the political climate in which they toiled.

Each was addressing the ways that the analyst would become an impediment to the analytic process, either in their own wishes to cure the patient or other related matters. Each was concerned with the problems of prosaic, over-formulated varieties of responsiveness to their patient. They were looking for fresh, creative forms of responsiveness that involved waiting and resisting obvious and more accessible types of interpretation. Each, in their unique ways, was developing Freud's discovery of free-floating attention.

Hinshelwood has suggested that Bion's (1967) statement of "without memory and desire" was in some ways indelicate since Bion was using the Eliot quote in a somewhat general, unnuanced manner. Bion had always considered that the analyst's attitudes and ideas are evolving during the analytic process. Thus, the analyst is striving toward "without memory and desire" but is by no means easily ever to be without it.

It is also possible that Winnicott (e.g., 1971, 1956, 1945), who had written extensively about the mother and analyst as actual objects, took exception to some of Bion's later writing about reverie, which seems to lay claim to ideas about the analyst's actual function as a receptor-organ during the process of reverie. Aguayo (2018) has discussed Winnicott's abundant frustration with Wisdom's presentation of Bion's work on reverie and the actuality of the object analyst/mother (Rodman, 1987, p. 14). Winnicott was upset that Bion's work was presented as if it was original, a claim that is apparent in an angry letter that Winnicott wrote to Wisdom in 1964. In the letter, Winnicott states

> Bion uses the word reverie to cover the idea that I have stated in the complex way that it deserves that the infant is ready to create something, and in "good enough" mothering, the mother lets the baby know what is being created. I don't mind being shown to be wrong or criticized or banged about. But I have done some important work out of the sweat of my psycho-analytic brow (i.e. clinically) and I refuse to be scotomized. (Rodman, 1987, p. 146)

Naturally, the tone of this letter as early as 1964 suggests that Winnicott was already prepared to greet Bion's ideas about "without memory and desire" with potential resentment. It seems that Winnicott was already upset that Bion was receiving attention for his discussion of the analyst as an actual object, a level of attention that Winnicott felt he had not received for his earlier work. Now, in his without memory and desire paper, whether Winnicott was correct or not, it may have seemed to Winnicott that Bion was less oriented to the actuality of the object and more toward a more dispassionate object. Bion went to some length to describe how for the analyst's responsiveness to be useful to the patient, it must hold different elements of the analyst's inner life. Still, it may have been a bit dizzying for Winnicott. Further, as Aguayo (2018) repeatedly noted in relation to a number of Bion's writings, Winnicott may have felt that Bion appropriated some of Winnicott's ideas about environmental influence without attributing credit to him for these ideas. This appropriation may have been further confounding for Winnicott given that at times Bion (e.g., 1949) may have noted the presence of the actual object but focused more on the "patient's phantasmic experience of the external object." While Winnicott was not insensitive to how this process might occur, it was not his focus on the external object in a number of papers that focused on the actuality of the object (e.g., Winnicott, 1945, 1951, 1956).

I will now briefly touch on a few other areas that might shed light on Winnicott's reactions to Bion's lecture, namely his view of maternal preoccupation; his view of playing and creative aggression related to the use of the object and the object's survival; and finally, his view of interpretation.

The Relevance of Maternal Preoccupation, Holding, and the Actuality of the Object

Winnicott (1945, 1956) argues that maternal preoccupation is based on the notion that the mother, "for the time being," is devoted to the care of her infant. At one level, the mother must recognize "absolute dependence on the mother and of her capacity for primary maternal preoccupation, or whatever it is called, is something which belongs to extreme sophistication, and to a stage not always reached by adults" (p. 304). Yet Winnicott repeatedly emphasized in his writing the need for the mother to be aware of her own limits and for the analyst to do so as well. I have suggested elsewhere that even the phrase "for the time being" suggests the mother's limits in her ability to be preoccupied (e.g., Cooper, in press).

To the extent that we can extrapolate the mother's attention to the interpretive focus of the analyst, the kind of attention that Winnicott is emphasizing, both regarding preoccupation and her own limits, is driven by, and I don't believe is well characterized by, being without memory and desire. Put another way, for Winnicott, limit is continually constitutive of play, as is all interpretive responsiveness, and is driven by the need for survival (e.g., Cooper, 2019).

Winnicott uses the phrase "for the time being" in relation to the mother's fastened attention in both the maternal preoccupation paper and in his paper, "Primitive Emotional Development." It is a beautifully condensed linguistic turn about how desire is temporally arriving and disappearing in the context of parenting and analytic work. The notion of the maternal preoccupation being held for the time being is to some extent at odds with an ideal of being without memory and desire, paradoxically so since the mother's conscious attention to her infant preoccupies as her own attention to any other conscious desires recede. His phrase "for the time being" reveals the impossibility of this stance as an ongoing position. Winnicott views limit as intrinsic to the guardianship of the setting and constitutive of play as evidenced in his two-part opus on play (Winnicott, 1968a, 1968b) as well as in his writing about hate in the countertransference (Winnicott, 1949).

Similarly, during transitional object development, the parent needs to be aware of the child's need for the transitional object, protecting that the child will have access to it, but too perfect an attunement to the child's need for the transitional object may interfere with the child's ability to parse the difference between reality and hallucination (Winnicott, 1951). The good enough parent is devoted to honoring the illusory elements of an object that is both me and not/me; of understanding the need to contain ambivalence about separation both within the child and within the parent's affective experience; and appreciating that the child needs to understand the difference between hallucination and reality. The parent's desire, like the analyst's desire, may involve wishes to provide awareness of these needs by the child while holding the inevitability of failure along the way.

Playing with and without Memory and Desire

In play, one of Winnicott's versions of paradox related to the analyst's mandate (is this desire?) is that he is to find play, initiated by the patient or analyst, but not search too much for it. Also, the analyst is both the guardian/supervisor of play and a participant.

One of Winnicott's greatest contributions to psychoanalysis was his ability to view illusion so positively, as a generative force. For example, the analyst's ability to occupy a state where linear time is of no consequence involves an extraordinarily compassionate and creative capacity to work with illusion and wish (Winnicott, 1968b; Cooper, 2023, 2025). Winnicott is profoundly interested in reality, but illusion is required to more deeply interrogate what reality is all about. We can't exclusively understand reality by commenting on it through interpretation. Instead, living in illusory places in life and in analysis can help us see and experience reality in new ways.

I have been quite interested in playing in analytic work with adult patients as the theoretical undergirding for analytic process for a few reasons. Winnicott's genius regarding play lay in his understanding of the relationship between the actuality of objects and experience interacting with fantasy and potential space. As I have defined it, playing in analysis with adults involves making use of reverie in particular ways that enter more deeply into elements of transference and intersubjective engagement and enactment. This occurs through idiomatic expressions of unconscious fantasy, defense, and conflict expressed by the patient or analyst through their associations and reverie. At the same time, playing is ordinary, a part of the associative process.

The play model rests on a few overlapping assumptions with that of a focus on reverie and dreaming. Yet, in my view, play makes use of reverie, including irreverent, subversive activity that at times rests less on at least the immediate goals of metabolization and integration. At times, play grows out of paradoxically disruptive forays into unhappy stasis (e.g., repetitive patterns, defenses, and entrenched unconscious fantasy). Both the reverie and playing models aim to promote self-observation, but they may each have different purposes at play related to metabolization. Both playing and reverie involve the goals of promoting equipoise related to holding sovereign states.

I would suggest, however, that the analyst oriented toward play waits in Winnicott's sense of waiting (Winnicott, 1968b), but he or she waits with and without memory and desire. In the remainder of this chapter, I try to shed light on the nature of this waiting and the paradox of being with and without memory and desire.

Creative Aggression, the Use of the Object, and Proceeding without Memory and Desire

Archaeologists understood before psychoanalysts that the act of understanding, locating, and piecing together how people lived in other times is intrinsically a destructive act. Bion and Winnicott, in their own ways regarding the examination of psychic phenomena, revolutionized our sense of how destroying what exists can yield new levels of experience and, in the process, brought us two overlapping and very distinct views of creative aggression.

Bion's (1967) quote of T. S. Eliot's "Four Quartets," without "memory and desire," seen from the framework of creative aggression, was his statement that selected facts and overvalued ideas need to be questioned and often destroyed on the way to yielding something fresh for patient and analyst. He follows Shelley's (1840) trenchant remark about desire in "A Defense of Poetry" that "We want the creative faculty to imagine that which we know."

Regarding Winnicott's own notions of what efforts the analyst makes toward listening, there is merit to argue that Winnicott's (1969) main work on creative aggression was his view of psychoanalysis as a form of playing and his contribution to understanding the use of the object.

I view Winnicott's contribution to the understanding of how play is the logical undergirding of psychoanalytic process as a major contribution regarding the creative elements of destruction. In play, the "rules" that constitute transference-countertransference engagement are in some way in interpretive transit. Play manifested in the analysis of adult patients arrives through idiomatic language, an ordinary language that nevertheless creatively finds unconscious fantasy, defense, and transference phenomena, providing metacommentary on the repetitive and stagnant rules that govern these phenomena.

In his work on the use of the object, Winnicott described how destroying the object and the object's survival creates a more genuine capacity to appraise an actual object. In light of Winnicott's letter to Bion, I suggest that the object desires to survive. In object usage, the patient attempts to destroy the analyst but must find an analyst who is dedicated to his or her own survival. The analyst desires to survive both intrinsically for his own survival but also to facilitate the patient's movement from destruction to object usage. This process is predicated on Winnicott's (1969, p. 1244) statement that: "the object, if it is to be used must necessarily be real in the sense of being part of shared reality, not a bundle of projections."

The analyst's desire to survive rests on his actual existence as an object. In Winnicott's (1951) paper on transitional objects, he offered an intriguing statement, namely that the importance of the transitional object lies in its "actuality" as an object more than its symbolic value. He was stating that while the object's symbolic linkage to the maternal figure is important, the actuality of the object as an object outside the subjective self is essential to the actual negotiation of separation. Symbolically, the transitional object serves to mitigate separation anxiety, but the second part of the transitional object is its function to shepherd the child's exploration with the object world. What better object with which to explore actual objects than an object that at the very least holds a dual function – to mitigate separation as an object outside the child's control and also an object that exists in fantasy as an object that is partly in the child's possession.

For our purposes of considering Winnicott's reservations about Bion's use of the phrase, "without memory and desire," I think it is essential to consider a paradox that Winnicott (1969) holds regarding the simultaneity of the object as actual and symbolic in transitional object development. As an actual object, Winnicott cannot quite promise to be without memory and desire beyond intention. In my view, then, the word intention is meant to capture a way that he persists in the importance of the interaction between the analyst as an actual and symbolic object, holding each side in paradoxical tension with the other.

In their unique ways, both Winnicott and Bion were contributing to creative versions of the concept of destruction in post-WWII England. The use of creative destruction in development for Winnicott was crucial to his development of the concept of the use of the object and to his theory of playing as the underlying logic for psychoanalysis. The object only becomes real if destroyed. One can speculate that Bion's recommendation to be without memory and desire is a kind of destruction of the object (memory and desire). However, in his letter to Bion, Winnicott might be suggesting that his experience of himself as an analytic object includes some elements of his memory and desire and, of course, that his patient's memory and desire are necessary in the process of living experiences together in the analytic process. We also know, thanks to Aguayo's (2014, 2018) nuanced reading of Bion that Bion's notion of "without memory and desire" points to Bion's (1967) appreciation that there is an evolution of the analyst's memory that includes realistically necessary and often helpful retention of what has happened in prior sessions. The notion of a constantly evolving position of without memory and desire in Bion's clinical listening may, in fact, be consistent with Winnicott's description of his own stance.

For Bion, we can derive a kind of creative destruction in the analyst's efforts to strive toward being without memory and desire. The questioning of certainty and Bion's (1973) quoting of Blanchot that "the answer is the misfortune of the question" led to a view of the creative elements tearing down particularly easily arrived at insights. This includes the analyst's receptivity to his or her disruptions in the capacity to think and disturbances in attunement.

We see how in both Winnicott and Bion's versions of the destruction of the object through playing and reverie, each was searching for frontiers that went beyond what was more accessible through formulation. They are each discovering their idioms of playing and reverie for learning from their patients' unconscious experiences. They each hold the analyst responsible for finding playing and dreaming when the patient is unable to play and dream.

While we see some of the roots of ontological analysis here, I hasten to add that I increasingly question the value of distinguishing between the epistemological and ontological axes. For example, Freud cannot be clearly specified as an epistemologically oriented analyst. Consider that when he discovered free-floating attention, he was trying to accompany his patients in a new way, albeit to arrive at new insights. Still, his efforts to unlearn his training that had asked of him to fix and solve symptoms involved a great deal of work to be present with his patients in a different way. Further still, his views on mourning as continuous rather than discrete suggest his burgeoning attunement to psychoanalysis and living as a process that could not always demarcate definite goals and ending points.

Winnicott's Interpretive Stance: Where Is the Analyst's Desire Located?

The texts I will refer to here include the enigmatic Chapter 4 in *Playing and Reality*, "Playing, Creativity, and the Search for the Self," written in 1967 (1968b), one part of Winnicott's two-piece opus on play, his tour de force paper on interpretation (Winnicott, 1968c); and "The Use of the Object" (Winnicott, 1969).

On the face of it, Winnicott's approach to interpretation, one that gathered over the course of his career, was to avoid anything that hinted at indoctrination of the patient. He is very aligned with Bion's concern about overdeveloped formulations and the possibility that interpretations are pseudo-integrative rather than honoring the particular state of disintegration that any patient might be in at any given moment.

In his paper on playing and creativity (Winnicott, 1968b), Winnicott is in a sense living in an illusory world of a patient who wishes for a session of indefinite length. He offers his patient a once-a-week treatment of three hours ("the best that I could manage") that is eventually modified into a two-hour session. One could say that his desire is expressed in the construction of the setting. He is giving himself over to the illusion that there is a session of indefinite length when, in reality, it is decidedly a session of defined length. His desire is to not interrupt the me/not me possession of the patient's view of the setting, particularly by interpreting it in all of the obvious ways that we as psychoanalysts are trained to do.

Winnicott's desire is to gather up the patient's bits and pieces and not get ahead of what he refers to as the patient's "transference confidence" (Winnicott, 1968c). Put succinctly, his desire is to promote the patient's discovery of elements of her creativity. We could say that his desire is in the waiting. Waiting here relates to a degree of trust that the patient will make her own discoveries, perhaps Winnicott's own version of faith.

In some ways, I believe that Winnicott's waiting is related to what the French philosopher Bernard Stiegler (2019) referred to as taking care. He plays on the French word *attendre*, to wait, but it includes attending. Stiegler refers to waiting as a waiting for the disclosure of webs of connectedness in oneself or in the other. It is a kind of mirroring. I see this as very similar to the very active waiting that Winnicott was describing.

Winnicott's waiting also relates to his notion that the analyst's job, when patients are unable to play, is to help find play. Here, it seems to me, is another element of the analyst's desire, not just a job description. Playing involves an openness to the kind of leap that Erikson and Plato associated with play. If nothing else, it is a usage of reverie and a different stage of interpretation that includes the analyst's registration of transference history with the patient in what often feels new.

If we think of Winnicott's waiting as related to Bion's trust in listening without memory and desire, here I would ask how or whether playing and reverie diverge a bit. Playing makes constant use of the analyst's reverie (e.g., Parsons, 1999; Cooper, 2018). Does playing involve an openness to the kind of leap that Erikson and Plato associated with play? If nothing else, playing involves a preliminary usage of reverie that leads to a different stage of interpretation, one that includes the analyst's registration of transference history with the patient in what often feels new.

It is my sense that play enters a listening position slightly less devoted to metabolization than that of reverie. Perhaps it could also be said that the aims of playing and reverie are overlapping and different. Winnicott's version of playing asks the patient and analyst to try to hold incompatible parts of self in an ongoing state of good enough unintegration. For Winnicott, the bits and pieces are searching less for equanimity but instead a sense of real and alive conversation with one another. I am not sure that metabolization is the most useful way to describe the function of play, even though play does help us to parse what is inside and outside.

Having described this particular state of unintegratedness in playing, I believe that this new state of responsiveness in playing is often mistakenly referred to as spontaneity. Spontaneity itself includes illusory experiences in the transference-countertransference because it builds on the evolving intersubjective history between patient and analyst. We could say that it builds on a history of memory and desire that has been held in abeyance as the analyst waits.

Regardless of the complex set of personal circumstances that prompted this letter, I am reminded of the importance that each analyst finds their own idiom to describe their responsiveness and participation in clinical analysis. I have emphasized a series of paradoxes in Winnicott's clinical stance that illuminate his objection to "without memory and desire." Winnicott's waiting is likely highly overlapping with Bion's instruction to listen without memory and desire. In that particular way, Winnicott's letter expresses the irrepressible need for each of us to be our own analyst.

References

Aguayo, J. (2014) Bion's notes on memory and desire – Its initial clinical reception in the United States: A note on archival material. *Int. J. Psycho-anal.* 95: 889–910.

Aguayo, J, (2018) Winnicott, Melanie Klein, and W. R. Bion: The controversy over the nature of the external object-holding and container/contained (1941–1967). *Psychoanal. Q.* 87: 767–807.

Bion, W. (1967) Notes on memory and desire. *Psychoanal. Forum* 2: 272–280.

Bion, W. (1970) *Attention and Interpretation.* London: Karnac Books.

Bion, W. (1973) Tavistock Seminar 3, 1977. In *Collected Works of Bion* 9: p. 33

Bonaminio, V. (2012) On Winnicott's clinical innovations in the analysis of adults. *Int. J Psycho-Anal.* 93: 1475–1485.

Bromberg, P. (1998) *Standing in the Spaces: Essays on Clinical Process, Trauma, and Dissociation.* Hillsdale, NJ: Analytic Press.

Cooper, S. H. (2018) Playing in the darkness: The use of the object and use of the subject. *J. Amer. Psychoanal. Assn.* 66: 743–765.

Cooper, S. H. (2023) *Playing and Becoming in Psychoanalysis.* London: Routledge.

Cooper, S. H. (2025) *Psychoanalysis in Play. Expanding Psychoanalytic Concepts from a Play Perspective.* London: Routledge.

Ogden, T. H. (2016) Destruction reconceived: On Winnicott's 'The use of an object and relating through identifications'. *Int. Psychoanal.* 97(5): 1243–1262.

Parsons, M. (1999) The logic of play. *Int. J. Psychoanal.* 80: 871–884.

Rodman, R. (1987) *The Spontaneous Gesture: Selected Letters of D. W.*, ed. F. R. Rodman. Cambridge, MA: Harvard University Press.

Shelley, P. B. (1840) *A Defense of Poetry and Other Essays.* London: Edward Moxen.

Steigler, B. (2019) *The Age of Disruption: Technology and Madness in Computational Capitalism.* Cambridge: Polity Press.

Winnicott, D. W. (1945) Primitive emotional development. *Int. J. Psychoanal.* 26: 137–143.

Winnicott, D. W. (1949) Hate in the countertransference. *Int. J. Psychoanal.* 30: 69–74.

Winnicott, D. W. (1956) Primary maternal preoccupation. In *Psychoanalytic Explorations,* ed. C. Winnicott, R. Shepherd, and M. Davis. Cambridge, MA: Harvard University Press, pp. 183–189.

Winnicott, D. W. (1967) Letter to W. Bion. In *The Collected Works of D. W. Winnicott: Volume 8, 1967,* ed. L. Caldwell and H. T. Robinson. Oxford: Oxford Academic, pp. 157–158.

Winnicott, D. W. (1968a) Interpretation in psycho-analysis. In *The Collected Works of D. W. Winnicott: Volume 8, 1967,* ed. L. Caldwell and H. T. Robinson. Oxford: Oxford Academic, pp. 253–258.

Winnicott, D. W. (1968b) Playing: A theoretical statement. In *The Collected Works of D. W. Winnicott: Volume 8, 1967,* ed. L. Caldwell and H. T. Robinson. Oxford: Oxford Academic, pp. 299–312.

Winnicott, D. W. (1968c) Creativity activity and the search for the self. In *Playing and Reality,* ed. L. Caldwell and H. T. Robinson. London: Tavistock, pp. 53–64.

Winnicott, D. W. (1969) The use of the object. *Int. J. Psycho-Anal.* 50: 711–716.

5 Play and Temporality in Psychoanalysis

A Close Reading of "Playing, Creativity, and the Search for the Self" in Winnicott's *Playing and Reality*

In this chapter, I will provide a personal interpretation of Winnicott's treatment of time throughout his writing. In particular, I provide a close reading of a complex and somewhat enigmatic paper by Winnicott, one of his two-part opus on play, Chapter 4 of *Playing and Reality*. In doing so, I will also link this crucial Winnicott paper with other Winnicott contributions to the understanding of temporality in "Fear of Breakdown" and "The Maternal Preoccupation." In "Fear of Breakdown" (Winnicott, 1974), a tour de force piece, Winnicott challenges our sense of futurity by helping us understand the past. Playing enters this matrix in a few ways that I will try to illuminate.

The close reading I attempt also overlaps with the purpose of the next chapter, namely to explore how, in my view, play always involves dimensions of temporality. I maintain that temporality is a vitally important element of the analytic setting, an experience of being alive, mourning, and finding a creative self. I am interested in playing in time.

Play and the setting of analysis relate to time in a few different ways. In the setting of analysis, the patient's time and analyst's time are in sync, out of sync, aligned, and misaligned. In some sense, place and time for Winnicott are inextricably linked, as I will explore. Winnicott's views on the setting are revealed in many sources, including "Hate in the Countertransference," both papers on play, his paper on interpretation in psychoanalysis, and early on in "Primitive Emotional Development."

"Playing, Creativity, and the Search for the Self": A Personal Reading

Winnicott's paper (1971) "Playing, Creativity, and the Search for the Self" is the second leg of Winnicott's two-piece opus on play, his revolutionary discovery that play is the logical undergirding of the analytic process itself. This is fundamentally a paper about play, inside play, and play so often involves time, the loss of time or object, specifically what I have referred to as the play of mourning.

Consider that for Winnicott, there is a box of temporality which resides inside or is inextricably bound with his notion of place. And they are both contained in the setting, a setting that allows for the emergence of play and creative experiences of self.

DOI: 10.4324/9781003569985-6

Winnicott repeatedly reminds us as readers of a collision between timelessness and real time, often bringing us back to the analysis of his patient in real time. He is every so often juxtaposing reality ("We are one hour or two hours into the session now") with the illusory, play realm of infinite or indefinite time. Put another way, playing and reality, unlimited and limited, infinite and finite, are always in play with one another.

Let's begin with Winnicott's opening:

> She had had a long treatment on a five-times-a-week basis for six years before coming to me, but found she needed a session of indefinite length, and this I could manage only once a week. We soon settled down to a session of three hours, later reduced to two hours. (p. 76)

Winnicott uses the term "settled" which expresses his effort to grasp the patient's unusual request. Here, Winnicott is giving us his first example of play in the work. The patient ound that she "needed a session of indefinite length and this I could manage only once a week." This is sort of funny. It is a kind of well-intentioned, compassionate, postured glibness on Winnicott's part. He could only manage a wish for indefinite time once a week. It is funny because it suggests the collision between infinite and finite. It is also funny because he uses the verb "manage" to describe trying to address the complexity of the wish for infinitude in the finite, actual hour. He brings us into the rules of play that the patient introduces to him. She is saying, "please work with my illusion here about my wish to construct the setting and control time." Winnicott implicitly replies, "Yes, I will work with your illusion but I can only do so once a week." Their analysis is off and running, juxtaposing infinite and finite, potential and limit in their challenging paradoxical equipoise.

In an unarticulated, unknowing manner, the patient is at the edges of disappointment and loss regarding the gap between a session of indefinite length and once a week, but they are playing that they have created a setting that will work. Indeed, it does involve settling into it, but it also brings up the full-throated, extraordinary possibility of mourning from the onset of analysis, the play of mourning. The patient is not yet born psychically, but she and they are already mourning in the temporal condensation arrived at later of birthday and deathday.

When Winnicott describes that she *found* she needed a session of indefinite length, he is telling us about the illusory structure that allows the patient to unconsciously hold a *promise* to be found (Winnicott's version of futurity). He will try to accompany her as she is finding herself, distinguished from the notion that he will try to find her. He is holding futurity in honoring the illusion that she found what she needed, knowing that it is a promise, a wish to be found. She found something. For Winnicott, unlike Loewald (1972), futurity, in some sense, lies in the setting more than in interpretation. It offers the possibility for psychic growth, for the birth of subjectivity where it has not already developed. Loewald focuses so beautifully on this element of futurity in each interpretation itself. These are important differences at the heart of an epistemological analysis and an ontologically based analysis that I will develop more a bit later.

Winnicott's way of putting it is also colloquial, and he is tipping his hat to us that he's not going to be an analyst who analyzes what this wish on her part is about, at least not yet. First, some of it is out of reach for each of us.

Regarding the play of temporality, illusion, and play, perhaps Winnicott is suggesting that, *for the time being*, he won't be making more conventional interpretation related to the meaning of his patient's wishes. I use the term *for the time being* because he is suggesting that for his patient to be as present as possible in time, he will resist interpreting unconscious fantasy. It is what Winnicott referred to in his paper on interpretation (Winnicott, 1968b) as not wanting to get ahead of the "transference confidence." I will take up what I refer to as "for the time being" later in this chapter.

It is likely that Winnicott had many ideas about her request, having been trained quite a bit to think this way. He is working to do something different, just as Bion's push to be without memory and desire involved another version of trying to push away these formulations or to plunge them into psychic crisis.

Rather than focusing on obvious elements of the patient's unconscious wishes, her aggression in tearing apart the setting, or elements of compromise formation, he is of the mind that understanding and finding are at this initial moment somewhat incompatible. I am reminded of a moment that Ogden (2022) recently described of a patient who, as she enters the office for the first session, says that she was very anxious coming over here. Ogden tells us that he said: "Of course you were." He is not understanding what made her anxious. He is helping her to feel found even if they will discover later that this quality of being found was illusory or temporary. They might do some understanding later. She might say, "Bullshit, you don't know me." But he is announcing his effort to live in a real and illusory place of being with rather than understanding, at least in this opening moment.

Here, time comes in since there is an imagined "later." There is the possibility of a promise of what comes later, which might even involve where someone has been. "You came in here from the storm." For now, questions like "What was it like? Who was with you in the storm?" are on hold. It is now of more concern that you are here now. You found yourself wanting a session of indefinite length. "Come in, I'll give you shelter from the storm." Winnicott was attempting to endure and bear not knowing with his patient who asks for a session of indefinite length.

Now, let's go further with how time and play are in dialogue with one another. Winnicott's response to the unnamed patient's request about time is to receive her communication as a protean effort at play and to engage in play with us as readers. He knows that a session of "indefinite" length can only be created in the place of play in which rules are made up as we go along. Winnicott doesn't want us to narrow our focus on a Stephanie, Betty, or Susan. It is fascinating that he names his child patients but not his adult patients. We are engaged in a form of play in which the rules governing transference-countertransference will be overturned. Illusions will be held, despite their treatment having a definite structure, because the structure has some shades of her creation. They are playing with the modes of indefinite, eternity, limit, in Ogden's (2024) terms, synchronic and diachronic time.

Throughout the chapter, Winnicott invites us on a journey in time. He asks us not to accept knowledge as something coming from the outside or something that is self-evident. He states: "Let me try to convey the feeling of what it is like to do work with this patient. But I must ask the reader to exert patience, much as I needed to be patient when engaged in this work" (p. 76). Winnicott asks us to think of time as a form of play and to give ourselves over to their shared illusions regarding time. And look at the play of Winnicott's language. The words, patience and patient used in the same sentence, are the linguistic enactment of his efforts to be a patient, to be with his patient, as he told us so often, to be both a participant and a supervisor of play. Steinbock (2024), in a cogent reading of this chapter, puts it so well when she states that, "In that sense her time is his time, there is no distinction." There is of course a distinction in Winnicott's mind, but he is telling us about his effort to not make it so, to enter into illusory space. He is trying to get as close as he can to something undefined about limit, but it all relies on the bedrock importance of limit in his views of the setting.

Steinbock (2024) also notes, as Winnicott repeatedly enters into the illusion of no limit in this treatment, that "Faith is required to simultaneously hold knowledge of objective time, reality, on the one hand, and the experience of infinite time, in an undifferentiated psychic matrix." In this faith, Steinbock is noting Winnicott's trust in the psyche's possibilities for growth.

The kind of faith that Steinbock is describing can actually only occur within a setting containing limits, a concept central to Winnicott's theory. In contrast, I am reminded of a view of love of the kind that Hannah Arendt (1961, 1996) and St. Augustine put forward in their own deeply ontological philosophies. Arendt's definition of love was: "I want you to be." "I want you to be" as a statement has no explicit limit or sign of contingency. In psychoanalysis, the commitment to promote a sense of being and personhood is always in play with our limitations regarding how much we are really capable of wanting this for another person. The line here between faith and devotion is quite porous.

One of Winnicott's greatest contributions to psychoanalysis was his ability to view illusion so positively, as a generative force. The analyst's ability to occupy a state where linear time is of no consequence involves an extraordinarily compassionate and creative capacity to work with illusion. Winnicott is profoundly interested in reality, but illusion is required to more deeply interrogate what reality is all about. We can't exclusively understand reality by commenting on it through interpretation. Instead, living in illusory places in life and in analysis can help us see and experience reality in new ways.

Here it is important to keep in mind that, paradoxically, Winnicott is our most creative theorist regarding limits, a fact sometimes not well understood by readers who reduce his theory to a kind of simplistic holding. Limit is constitutive of play (Cooper, 2021). Here, the illusory element of the indefinite relies on the reality that this is most definitely a session of limited length. Like with the transitional object, Winnicott gives himself over to, even fostering the notion that the patient has created a session's length, not challenging its existence or the needs arising for it. So I also read his references to actual time in his conversation with us as readers as his awareness of the illusory elements of time that the treatment is making use of, as well as his necessary limits.

He wants to always remind us that play is juxtaposed with reality, and he does so throughout this chapter and opus. Faith here simultaneously holds both "synchronic and diachronic time" (Ogden, 2024). Winnicott wants us to hold a paradoxical reality of linear time having consequence and no consequence. He wrote autobiographically, "Oh, to be awake when I die." To have time to waste, we need the illusion that there is time to waste. I would say that the analyst occupies a space of paradoxical realities in which time is limited and unlimited.

I remind us again that in holding paradoxical realities, we are in play. That's what Winnicott is living with this patient even as he is the guardian of the setting. As the guardian of the setting, he sometimes says to her and to us, "Peek-a-boo, I see you." In the transference and in the illusory space of work, he is providing a setting that holds illusion and the possibility that something might happen when there is no obvious sign that something will happen.

Winnicott is undoubtedly working hard to create a new type of music with this patient, forcing himself to be quiet and not make clever interpretations, just as Bion is particularly interested in what the analyst needs to do within his own mind in fighting against familiar formulations and selected facts. Bion and Winnicott each introduced us to how inevitably we will become obstructions to the analytic process. Winnicott's narration of how much time has passed is also an allusion to his active work of giving himself over to his patient's subjectivized version of time. He is aware that we as readers are outside the analytic couple and still time-bound in the conventional sense of time. It can never be emphasized enough that Winnicott is always interested in reality. All play occurs as juxtaposed with reality. Playing is not the opposite of what is serious, but is real. Time is a plaything, an object of play in this clinical example.

And playing always involves time and the creative mixing up of past, present, and future. I think that Loewald (1961;1972) means something similar when he emphasizes that the experience of time refers to the interactions and interrelations between these three temporal modes of psychic activity, especially in the play of transference. Here, unconscious and conscious remembering and anticipating, and the interplay between primitive and higher-order motivations, are most striking.

Let's take another angle on Winnicott's version of time from his tour de force paper, largely ignored, "Interpretation in Psychoanalysis," written in the same year, 1968, as his two papers on play. This paper lives and breathes with his ideas about interpretation functioning to "gather in the patient's bits and pieces," a phrase that he began using in the 1950s and 1960s to describe our general, ongoing lack of integration. Parenthetically, it is interesting to me that Loewald borrows Winnicott's phrase in his paper on temporality. Winnicott wants to avoid pseudo-interpretations that presume nonexistent integration. He told us in this year that he views each of us as being in bits and pieces, that the ways that we think about integration are largely a shared illusion held by organized psychoanalytic theories, a kind of epiphenomenal illusion that is shared by organized psychoanalysis.

Winnicott's notion of bits and pieces, our lack of integration, was also a statement about our experience of time. Our bits and pieces are the minutes and seconds, the ticking clock that we can never fully integrate, and so let's not presume integrated states where they don't exist.

Winnicott's concept of gathering up as a function of interpretation is particularly important in a moment toward the end of the session that he is summarizing. Winnicott tells us that the patient reports how she often looks in the many mirrors in her room for someone who is looking at her, looking with her to mirror herself back to her. I was reminded of a memory that Truman Capote had of Marilyn Monroe when they were out to lunch one day. Monroe went to the ladies' room and was gone for quite a long time, so Capote went to check on her. He knocked on the door and entered, and Monroe was looking at herself in the mirror. He asked, "Marilyn, what are you doing?" She replied, "I'm looking at her."

The moment that Winnicott describes is one of essentially a gathering up by the patient of her own bits and pieces, and he acknowledges this when he says: "It was yourself that was searching," adding that he means that she exists in the NOW of searching rather than in the "someday and if only" (Aktar, 1996) of finding or being found (p. 85). It echoes Winnicott's most important statement in this chapter and one of his most important statements about play, "It is in playing and only in playing that the individual child or adult is able to be creative and to use the whole personality, and it is only in being creative that the individual discovers the self."

When Winnicott says to his patient: "You are living an experience, NOW," it can easily be seen as a sense of anticipating the patient's future. But I suggest that Winnicott is so allergic to indoctrinating the patient based on his own analytic training that Loewald's view of interpretation anticipating a psychic future is outside Winnicott's ken. Winnicott is saying to his patient: "You are living an experience, NOW."

Here, we arrive at one of the most complex areas of overlap and difference between Winnicott and Loewald related to the matter of futurity. As we know, Loewald appreciated that all interpretations take us one step into the psychic future just as they take us into a past, presumably an impulse that has led to defense that the interpretation is trying to illuminate. Winnicott's concern with indoctrinating the patient is in essence a concern with the potentially malignant sense of futurity that our hopes can have for some patients. Loewald considers that there is no such thing as an interpretation that is not suggestive, including, I imagine, his view of an embedded hope in Winnicott's ontologically oriented attempt to be with rather than speak about. Returning to Hannah Arendt's definition of love, "I want you to be," with a Loewaldian twist, it might go something like this: "I want you to be becoming. I have something that might help you in becoming." Winnicott says, as it were, "Sometimes, I see you becoming."

Steinbock's (2024) notion that "Faith *resides* in the psyche's healthy tendency to situate itself where possibility emerges" approximates a meaningful integration of the two ways of seeing. There is, however, value in remembering that Loewald and Winnicott's discussion of futurity is aimed at somewhat different levels of theoretical discourse. While Loewald (1960) emphasizes that all interpretations anticipate a psychic future, Winnicott is more focused on the gathering up of the patient's bits and pieces in the setting, not knowing where the patient is going but trusting the patient's capacity to grow.

In this sense, Loewald is a more modern theorist in relation to our ideas about the inevitability of suggestion than Winnicott. In my reading of Winnicott's version of play, Winnicott is holding on to an illusion of non-impingement. After all, play has radical implications related to suggestion that he never deconstructed theoretically, including performative elements and the intrinsic violence of all interpretation. It was there in all of his writing, but he never theorized it beyond his view of creative destruction in "The Use of an Object." It has been the subject of my own writing in recent years.

This Winnicott paper demonstrates so fully his repetitive claim in a dozen or so papers that he interprets to show his patients the limits of his understanding. For Winnicott, the impoverishment of interpretation is the offering, the being with that he wants us to feel good about offering. It is the same offering that Albert Camus makes to us when he states that we must conjure up that Sisyphus is happy in his endless activity. Or Beckett's now perhaps overworked but beautiful phrase that "to be human is to fail. Try to fail better." If we imagine putting together Loewald and Winnicott for a moment, imagining Loewald as a play theorist, Loewald is an expert at seeing the patient's protean efforts at play, the play that can anticipate a future before we can consciously grasp it. Winnicott holds disavowed hope in the limits of interpretation, while Loewald holds more hope in the accuracy of interpretation.

Thinking about the complexity of overlap and distinction between Loewald and Winnicott on temporality puts me in mind of a kind of unfortunate binary in our contemporary thinking regarding epistemological and ontological approaches to psychoanalysis, no matter how hard we fight it. It has been a theme that rears its head quite repeatedly in this book, and I hope that this book allows us to think about this matter in something other than either/or terms. For example, we know that while Bion and Winnicott created ontologically oriented analysis, we also know that standard types of defense and transference interpretations were a part of their work. I find that the modes of listening that Winnicott helps me move toward, often evolve from earlier, more standard forms of interpretive responsiveness. In fact, I believe that a valuable part of each analysis is the patient's experience of our trying and failing to understand, which is, after all, a kind of being with.

Furthermore, as I have suggested earlier in this volume, even Freud has strong elements of ontological thinking. His concepts of free-floating attention and his implicit listening position in the goals of analysis (to transform human misery into ordinary unhappiness) suggest that knowing ourselves will inevitably involve being with ourselves in new and abiding ways.

In creatively allowing ourselves to enter the illusion of infinite time or eternity, we need to keep in mind the possibility that nostalgia rears its head as we are brought into "someday" and "if only" fantasies. We hope that our patients can find reasons and motivation to make use of the illusion of infinite time. Winnicott's patient found her way out of it. There are patients who, unfortunately, use analysis to find more permanent refuge in fantasies of infinite time, infinite possibility, libidinizing a merger with a mother and child that never was. Here we are in the territory of the libidinization of the negative, of the dead mother, what I call the frozen memorialization of what never was.

I end with the observation that Winnicott's notion of temporality linked time and place as components of the birth of subjectivity. It is everywhere in Winnicott, most particularly in his seminal paper, "Primitive Emotional Development." We need a place in time to be, to have a subjectivity, and he is the cartographer of that developmental process, in time. We also need a place for going on being after the birth of subjectivity. Being alone in the presence of another is all about being in time, and his allusions to orgasm as transient, in time, in the capacity to be alone, are all about the density and simultaneity of eternity and finitude. Winnicott captured so beautifully the abracadabra of a session of indefinite length in one meeting per week. It is an essence of our illusions about the experience and interrogation of eternity and timelessness in analysis, juxtaposed with our mortality.

References

Aktar, S. (1996) Someday and if only fantasies: Pathological optimism and inordinate idealization as related forms of idealization. *J Amer Psychoanal.* 44: 723–753.

Arendt, H. (1961) *Between Past and Future*. London: Faber and Faber Limited.

Arendt, H. (1996) *Love and Saint Augustine,* ed. Joanna Vecchiarelli Scott and Judith Chelius Stark. Chicago, IL: The University of Chicago Press.

Cooper, S. H. (2021) Toward an ethic of play. *The Psychoanal. Q.* 90: 373–397.

Goldberg, P. (2024) On the discovery/creation of lived time: Discussion of Steinbock. *Psychoanal. Dial.* 34: 687–692.

Loewald, H. W. (1960) The therapeutic action of psychoanalysis. *Int. J. Psychoanal.* 41: 16–43.
Loewald, H. W. (1972) The experience of time. *Psychoanal. St. Child* 27: 401–410.
Loewald, H. W. Super Ego and Time (1961) *The Essential Loewald – Collected Papers and Monographs*. Hagerstown, MD: University Publishing Group, Inc., 2000.
Ogden, T. (2022) *Coming to Life in the Consulting Room: Toward a New Analytic Sensibility*. London: Routledge.
Ogden T. (2024) Rethinking concepts of the unconscious and analytic time. *Int. J. Psychoanal*. 105: 270–291.
Steinbock, S. (2024) Reflections on "A woman who found she needed a session of indefinite length": A look at chapter four of Winnicott's *Playing and Reality* through the prism of its modalities of temporality. *Psychoanal. Dialog*. 34: 676–688.
Winnicott, D. W. (1968a) Letter to W. Bion. In *The Collected Works of D. W. Winnicott*, ed. L. Caldwell and H. T. Robinson, Vol. 8. Oxford: Oxford Academic, pp. 211–213.
Winnicott, D. W. (1968b) The place where we live. In *The Collected Works of D. W. Winnicott*, ed. L. Caldwell and H. T. Robinson, Vol. 8. Oxford: Oxford Academic, pp. 221–227.
Winnicott, D. W. (1971) Creativity activity and the search for the self. In *Playing and Reality*. London: Tavistock.
Winnicott, D. W. (1974) Fear of breakdown. *Int. Rev of Psychoanal*. 1: 103–107.

6 Playing in Time

Some Reflections on Temporality in the Analytic Setting

In concert with the issues of "for the time being" and playing in time, I also consider intrinsic elements of waiting in the analytic situation. Waiting is an activity, not a passive position of simply holding back (Winnicott, 1968a; Slochower, 1996). And it need be said that holding back is itself an activity. Winnicott's (1968a) clinical elaboration of waiting was one of his greatest achievements because it embodied his sense of the impoverishment of interpretation. The concept of waiting for Winnicott is sneakingly theorized, far more complex than his writing would sometimes indicate. Finally, I will also consider how in some analyses, the patient's capacity and need to waste time is an essential part of therapeutic action. I will provide some clinical material that illuminates a few ways that I think about time in relation to the play of analytic work.

Since all playing occurs in time, what does it mean to suggest a phrase such as "playing in time"? I will suggest a few varieties of how play and time unfold in analytic work, such as playing "for the time being," playing with the illusion of endless time, and the experience of waiting in analysis.

Introduction

In earlier work, I suggested that most of play is framed in relation to loss (Cooper, 2018, 2019, 2023a, 2023b). Freud's discovery of fort da was just one example of that observation. Many childhood games of peek-a-boo and hide-and-seek all involve attempts to work with loss, whether it is the everyday loss of people coming and going, or more ongoing, profound separations. Parsons (1999) also provided an example in which he framed playing in the context of mourning.

Scarfone (2015) offers an extremely thoughtful approach to loss and its relationship to temporality in general. In exploring what he refers to as "the logic of loss," Scarfone suggests that loss shatters an illusory sense of being that is in some sense pre-temporal. Winnicott's sense of "going on being" is interrupted by loss or, even earlier, the growing awareness that objects, including the breast, exist outside our own being. In other words, we learn about time through discovering otherness since otherness, paradoxically, means that we lose a sense that we are everything. Scarfone (developing

DOI: 10.4324/9781003569985-7

some of Laplanche's (1997) (1999) notions of temporality) puts it as follows: "Time then steps in when the infant notices that there is a message from the other (despite its enigmatic nature) and tries to make sense of it, to translate it" (2015, p. 18).

Perhaps we could say that Winnicott's (1969) notion of survival of the object following the infant's destruction of the object involves the birth of temporality. When we can say to the object that we have destroyed, "hello object, I love you," we are being in time with that object. We are in a place and a time.

Regarding one axis of the temporal element in psychoanalysis, loss is situated in the more straightforward framework of before and after. We have something and then we don't, at least in material terms. The daily ritualistic process of analysis features this coming and going in a continuous way. In fact, the setting is characterized by the presence of the analyst with the patient for a session and then his or her absence when it ends. And similarly, the setting involves constant loss for the analyst as well.

Then there is the notion of timelessness in the analytic setting, a timelessness that is always juxtaposed with the finiteness of the setting. We are engaged in some activities in analytic work in which the timelessness of the unconscious is front and center. The transference mobilizes and vivifies the past in ways that make the present and past fused in the minds of the patient. Loewald (1972) featured how the past, present, and future are embodied in the transference. Loewald is always describing a density of time in which timelessness and the present are in dialectical relation to one another. Winnicott's (1971) Chapter 4 of *Playing and Reality* includes an example of how a patient feels, at once, her nonexistence with her parents from the past and how it is experienced in the present in the transference with her analyst. The patient makes movement from a stultified, forever sense of not being seen to an experience of herself searching in the presence of her analyst for a new present and future.

Ogden (2024) has distinguished between diachronic (clock time or measured time) versus synchronic time, which is dream time. Echoing Loewald (1972), Ogden suggests that the analytic situation is designed to help the patient live in synchronic time (dream time) in which patient and analyst attempt to dream together.

For much of the time in analytic work, it seems to me that we are living in illusory places regarding time that involve a range of experiences of time, with timelessness or eternity being just one. There is no such thing as a pure version of dream time nor of diachronic time. Patients and analysts are constantly moving back and forth in their associations and experience between the two modalities. Part of the analyst's guardianship of the setting involves his or her ability to hold the paradoxical nature of limited time (clock time with the beginning and end of the session) with the timelessness of the unconscious, namely the merger between past, present, and future embodied in transference-countertransference.

Psychoanalysis operates continuously with our illusions, involving playing with endings, limits, and the reality of the materiality of time. Patient and analyst are attempting to listen to the patient's unconscious in particular ways, "for the time being." Unless a patient is psychotic, they are often aware that when we are listening in particular ways for the time being, it is not the only way that we will listen to even the same stories and material over time.

This is not to say that the matter of holding complex experiences of illusion "for the time being" or the incompatible realities intrinsic to unconscious fantasy is an easy thing for any of us. In fact, the ability to hold paradoxical realities related to time and transference is often in some sense a goal of analytic work.

Even in the context of inevitable repetition, psychoanalysis is also nearly always about transit of one kind or another regarding holding paradox. I will try to capture some of the varieties of this transit through some brief clinical examples.

For the Time Being

Winnicott (1958) used the expression "for the time being" to describe the mother's maternal preoccupation during the early stages of her infant's life. It was described as a nearly psychotic state, one that would only actually be sustainable for a limited amount of time. It is understood as a near-psychotic state in that the mother's absorption involves selective attention to the needs of the infant while minimizing perceptions and experiences that are unrelated to the infant.

It seems to me that the concept of "for the time being" is generally quite applicable to many phases of analytic work. For the time being, we listen to obvious defensive operations of the patient and do or do not immediately interpret them. For the time being, we hear elements of unconscious fantasy that we register in our minds but don't necessarily take up with the patient. For the time being, we hear a few allusions to the transference but decide whether or not we will continue to work in displacement or take them up more directly.

In Chapter 4 of this volume, in my discussion of Winnicott's fourth chapter in *Playing and Reality*, I suggested that Winnicott's approach to the patient's request for a session of unlimited length was to honor the patient's illusion about the setting of analysis. Winnicott seems to have decided that, *for the time being*, the best that he could do was to offer a session of three hours in length and that the patient and he would be able to accept this structure as an approximation of a session of unlimited length. His statement that the session eventually moved into a shorter period of time suggests that the illusion being shared was able to shift over the course of analytic work into a session of more conspicuously limited length.

In a developmental context, it is essential for children to learn the importance of the concept "for the time being" in order to sustain frustration and to persevere in learning tasks. In the best of circumstances, they learn that hunger or helplessness shall pass. Hunger is satiated. Hopefully, a needed parent is good enough and can provide comfort in times of need or pain. The experience of "for the time being" is intrinsically related to the holding and containing parent. The good enough parent holds the illusion of the transitional object for the time being until the object and reality itself can be more fully appraised and accepted.

Implicit in this function of the containing other in the context of the time being is the notion of the object's limits. The parent must be willing to set limits on how long particular kinds of illusions will be held, lest the child never learns the difference between hallucination and reality (e.g., Winnicott, 1951). Analysts may decide to honor particular kinds of requests by a patient for the time being, especially related to the setting, but if it exceeds the analyst's limits, nothing analytic will happen.

The importance of the concept "for the time being" continues to be significant in the ongoing psychic challenges of being a person. In analysis, we learn that as we explore irrational and unconscious forces inside us, time is required. We discover the ways that we are *possessed* (Laplanche, 1997,1999) or *occupied* by alien forces (Kristeva, 1989), and this discovery involves patience and waiting. The process of seeing whether we are able to get more purchase on our unconscious minds is not predictable and certainly not reconcilable with more conventional versions of clock time.

In many ways, I believe that one of the most important therapeutic gifts of analytic work is the opportunity it affords us as adults to sustain the experience of "for the time being." For example, a patient comes into a session dumbfounded by some aspect of his unconscious mind, such as acting self-destructively or foolishly. His behavior has made him feel a bit out of control. It is unlikely that, over the course of the session, something will be "resolved" about this piece of behavior or the accompanying embarrassment, shame, or guilt. Yet the patient may have a sense by the end of the session that something about understanding himself or speaking about his behavior with his analyst is sustaining.

Patients learn to abide, to endure the refractoriness of their psychic lives, including some of the most vexing aspects of their unconscious minds. Laplanche (1997,1999), in describing what he termed Freud's Copernican revolution, emphasized that our unconscious minds involve a kind of "decentering," whereby the subject is no longer capable of feeling entirely in control of what S. Frosch (2002) referred to as the alien core inside us. Laplanche put it like this:

> The sharpness of Freud's vision is testified to by terms like "internal foreign body" or "reminiscence." They define the unconscious as an alien inside me and even put inside me by an alien. At his most prophetic, Freud does not hesitate over formulations which go back to the idea of possession. (1997, p. 658)

Similarly, Kristeva (1989) refers to the same set of processes as Laplanche through the word "uncanny."

Rather than evoke notions of mysticism, Kristeva is emphasizing the experience, the phenomenology of forces that feel as though they are acting from within.

Patients in analysis learn to accept that, for the time being, they are in periods of surrender to the ways in which they are partly under the sway of their unconscious minds. They always were, but analysis puts this into stark relief. Sometimes this acceptance, quite the opposite of resignation, is one of the great gifts of analytic work. It could be said that it marks a shift from "the time being" to "being in time," even if being in time involves waiting.

I suggest that the patient's experience of being accompanied by another person, the analyst, in a caring and deeply engaged way *for the time being,* promotes the capacity to *keep on going on being.*

The Activity and Transit of Waiting

One of the many experiences of "for the time being" in analysis is the exploration and honoring of these elements of possession and craziness so that they can be expressed and interrogated. An important element, along with exploring, is the implied waiting that occurs during this process. Patients who are waiting have someone waiting with them. This waiting is an active process, not sitting on one's hands as both patient and analyst. Waiting is sometimes a world of thoughts and fragmented meaning before we can live in a world of being and experiencing. It is a kind of emotional and aesthetic cluster where emotions gather and inhabit us, and where meaning and symbolization are not rushed, sometimes found, sometimes a short-lived or illusory finding, and perhaps sometimes not even found.

Winnicott (1968b) commented "that to be creative, a person must exist and have a feeling of existing" (p. 79). Winnicott was describing an unhurried place that is not cluttered with habitual modes of responding. It is a place from which we can find a modicum of emotional freedom.

The kind of waiting that is distinctly psychoanalytic and that Winnicott elaborated throughout his opus is always an active form of waiting. It led me to publish a paper several years ago, called "The Activity of Neutrality," a version of which is published in this volume (Chapter 2). In that chapter, I highlight the constant activity in all analytic processes.

All psychoanalytic concepts such as transference, countertransference, waiting, playing, and dreaming, even neutrality, involve activities, not nouns. There is no "the transference," "the countertransference," "the neutrality," "the play," or "the dream." We are always finding even as we wait.

For a moment, consider Beckett's monumental "Waiting for Godot." The play has been debated by literary critics since it was first performed in Paris. I am most drawn to an interpretation of its existential implications, namely that conscious reality is so complex partly because, in the absence of an objective reality, human beings are forced to create value by living. We are not capable of philosophizing or talking about reality in the mind, so we are forced to contend with the lack of intrinsic purpose in human existence. We create value by living, perhaps the best example of the activity in waiting.

Since Winnicott and Bion, we have come to appreciate that waiting in psychoanalysis is contrasted with filling our minds and our patients' minds with meaning. Waiting is a process that is not only about waiting for meaning to come from the patient or analyst. Waiting is a kind of openness to experience, a waiting that facilitates the individual patient coming to terms with their own lived and living experience.

Naturally, we as analysts have many ways in which we can contribute to that process. Waiting is often not the same as not speaking. Waiting is an attitude in which there is an embedded respect for the patient's ultimate task of valuing what they feel, think, and desire.

The "passion in waiting" (another quote from T. S. Eliot that Independents emphasize, e.g., King, 1973) resides in a respect for the genuine trust that something will "turn up" (Winnicott, 1968a) that feels meaningful to the patient.

Helping patients develop the capacity to wait is embedded in multiple theories of psychoanalysis: the taming and neutralization of drives in Freudian and ego psychologies; the integration of libidinally and aggressively tinged object relations and representations in Fairbairn, Klein, and Kernberg; the theory of the depressive position itself is, in many ways, about developing the capacity for genuine, deep waiting; and waiting is expressed in Bion's admonition for us to wait without memory and desire, more specifically to resist the obvious formulations and selected facts as we listen, in order to wait for something fresh to appear.

But no theorist addressed the theory of waiting and a theory of waiting as an activity for both patient and analyst as did Winnicott. Winnicott's (1968a) paper, "Interpretation in Psychoanalysis," describes in great detail how he thinks about waiting in psychoanalysis. It is the outgrowth of 20 earlier years of his own and other Independent tradition analytic writings about the pivotal role of waiting as intrinsic to how interpretation attempts to gather up the patient's bits and pieces and to find play (Winnicott, 1968b).

The purpose of waiting is illuminated by thinking about temporality in analytic work. It seems to me that the most effective kinds of interpretations are those in which something about the past and present has come together. There is often a kind of experiential transit between the past and present. The patient feels and remembers things from the past, and they are experiencing things that are related now within themselves and with the analyst. There is a density of the experience of time in psychoanalytic waiting (e.g., Loewald, 1972; Bonowitz, 2021). The activity of waiting involves being simultaneously in different time zones, as it were.

To me, the most interesting kind of waiting in analysis is the way in which patient and analyst are spectators to what I have termed a crime scene

(Cooper, 2014). The crime scene is often the architecture of the patient's survival of their family and the family rules that govern his adaptation and that the patient will institute as the rules of transference-countertransference engagement in his analysis (e.g., Symington, 1983).

The analyst must abide by these adaptations and learn how to wait with his patient in order to see what will emerge from the crime scene. There is much play here of various kinds. For example, mourning our most constraining attachments requires patient and analyst to appreciate and abide by the aesthetics of the patient's jury-rigged adaptations. We have all had some of our most poignant and sometimes even humorous moments with our patients admiring how twisted our adaptations are, how wasteful too, before we can let go of them a bit. Each of us as patients is an artist of our affliction, and we as analysts are trained to appreciate this art. This appreciation sometimes emerges in forms of play related to mourning (e.g., Parsons, 1999; Cooper, 2023a).

Of course, these moments of admiring our patients' neuroses with them as a form of play run the risk of being glib. Instead, I think of it as a way that we abide how important and creative these constructions really are. *We are required to understand the importance of these adaptations from the past in the present.* Unless the patient can feel our sense of understanding how essential these adaptations, that still feel real and necessary, are, we able to have traction for helping them to experience something new.

Regarding the elegance of our adaptive afflictions, Julia Kristeva (1989) stressed that in order to express pain, one cannot allow the style to be completely harmonious. As she put it, "Stylistic awkwardness is discourse of dulled pain" (p. 27).

Waiting is also a good metaphor for containment of all the unrealized fantasies that are a part of every individual's inner life. Waiting is a kind of abiding that patients learn. Abiding is one of the most important functions that analysts carry out for their patients and that some patients learn to internalize.

I believe that analysis involves finding some of our worst experiences and bad internal objects as better play partners than they were before analysis (e.g., Cooper, 2023b). This involves a kind of waiting on the patient's part, a waiting that accepts that many of these experiences will recede but not entirely disappear.

Another element of waiting and "for the time being" is a series of implicit requests that patients make of us, often involving enacting various kinds of conflicts. Consider a patient who is a highly accomplished academician struggling with writing a new book. She described in one session a series of stories about how much her mother confabulated as she was growing up, often weaving a story about her and her sister while not knowing who they were. My patient and I began to understand that inhibiting her writing was a kind of preemptive strike in which it would hurt less to not be seen if she did the editing and inhibiting rather than write the book and not be seen by her mother. My patient was, in her symptom, in a waiting mode to be seen that was safer than if she were to write. In waiting, hesitating, she felt safer than risking the possibility of being a nuisance by asking for her mother's likely unavailable attention. She was waiting for something that had never happened and showed no promise of happening, namely to be seen by her mother.

In her analysis, it took me a period of time before I could identify ways that the patient was enacting a wish for me to do something rather than for her to do something. Eventually, we were able to examine how she was waiting for me to do something for her rather than finding parts of herself that might be able to change and take on risk.

Interestingly, it was in my waiting that I could help my patient to understand her waiting of a different kind. Her waiting was the expression and enactment of a wish to be seen and heard in a way that was new for her, a way that she might more genuinely experience going on being. My waiting, in contrast, involved a kind of trust that we could speak about these matters in less intellectualized and disembodied ways if we found some genuine experiences together that brought the past and present together in time.

In psychoanalysis, I conceptualize waiting as a form of play like everything else in psychoanalysis. Waiting may be seen as a kind of limit, a bedrock element of reality. It marks the analyst's limits of understanding and that understanding occurs in time and over time. This is what patients in psychoanalysis need to learn to do, and this is what psychoanalysts need to learn to do. There is a great deal of play and resistance to play that occurs in relation to these limits for both patient and analyst.

Waiting as a defense, one that Winnicott emphasized in "Fear of Breakdown," is the waiting for something that has already happened. We are living in the trauma of knowing that we are waiting for something dreadful that has happened to our families, our ancestors, and our community. Waiting is inextricably linked to the fear that we will be waiting forever. It also leads us to the question: Do I really have to take responsibility for knowing what I already know? The question shows us the ragged edges of the struggle, the hypersigns in Julia Kristeva's terms of loss and mourning. Why must it be so? Perhaps even: Do I have to die? Are we there yet?

Waiting in psychoanalysis involves the complicated fact that at any given moment, we are already there. Where you are, the way you are being and feeling, is the way you are and the way you are being. What you are saying and how you are being reflects something important and interesting about who you are now. We always have to propose that we interrogate how interesting waiting really is and can be. Free association and free-floating attention allow us to see what we are waiting for.

The question "Are we there yet?" is a kind of resistance. It is one that teeters on the exquisite edge between knowing a reality, a reality that we aren't there yet (and in fact, we often already know how many miles and how many minutes we are actually away), and wanting to indulge in the magical fantasy that an omnipotent other can take away the waiting. This waiting is the art of integrating reality.

When we ask the question "Are we there yet?," we must always consider that perhaps you are already someplace that you don't want to be, something has already happened but which we can now face with more courage and support. In other words, "Yes, we are indeed there. Now the question is where can we go from here." That's the kind of waiting that we learn how to love in psychoanalysis, and it is a waiting worth waiting for.

Freeze-Framing and Waiting

We can never know what the question "Are we there yet?" means without considering the listener. Our ability as analysts to wait is the precondition to helping others to wait. An impatient psychoanalyst or exhausted parent hears the question with more annoyance. Sometimes analysts and parents are able to translate the question into something interesting about where they already are. Something like:

> You're so concerned about "someday and if only" (Akhtar, 1996) that the now of your experience, the town that you and I are traveling through, the song we're listening to, the thoughts and associations that you are having as a patient, the argument that you are having with your sister, the experience of needing to pee, are all kind of interesting in their own right.

So many of the ways that we help patients to be in the time they are in, or to tolerate feelings for the time being, involve slowing things down or providing a kind of freeze-framing of the time that we are in. Sometimes when I begin to say something to a patient about what I've heard, it is almost as if I am saying, de facto, "for the time being let's freeze this moment and see what we see," or "let's see what you feel," or sometimes, "let's see what you might have been saying that you weren't aware that you were saying."

A young adult patient began her hour with the observation that she never had preferences about what she and her family should do when they were on vacation together. She associated to how her older brothers were always arguing on family vacations in a way that made her anxious. She wanted to run away. She described not being able to think at these times. She then associated to her parents' fights and how, again, she wanted to be elsewhere. In many ways, the session became a place to think and feel within that space as I showed her repeatedly how she moved away from thinking about what she wanted. My attempts to freeze-frame these moments with her family provided a kind of auxiliary setting for thinking in ways that she was unaccustomed to.

Waiting in these contexts involves not knowing what will occur for unspecified time. This patient was uncertain about the value of thinking about what she wanted, even though I felt that she was aching for such an opportunity. She was often incredulous about affording herself to think about what she wanted, and my efforts were partly in the service of providing a setting, being a guardian of the setting, so that she might be able to do this in a new way.

Time Wasted, Time Found

For some patients, one of the most pleasurable illusions in psychoanalytic work is the illusion that analysis will just keep rolling along. For reasons that are not entirely clear to me, it seems as though analyses in the United States keep getting longer and longer. There are also patients who say that they would like to never stop analysis and some analysts who seem to feel similarly. While the meaning of that sentiment obviously varies from patient to patient and across varying patient/analyst dyads, it does seem as though there is a trend of some kind toward far longer analyses.

Speculating from the seat of my pants, I wonder whether part of that shift might relate to an ontological trend in analytic work. If the emphasis of analytic work is less organized around knowing oneself, and there is more emphasis on living creatively with oneself and others, then it may seem more artificial to leave a relationship that continually facilitates that process. In some ways, we have moved further away from a model of a treater and a patient and more to models of "companioning" (e.g., Grossmark, 2018).

In my experience, there is a distinction to be made between the patient making use of the analyst, even in what I am calling, "having time to waste mode," versus a sense of the analyst as doing nothing but submitting to the patient's demands about holding on to a relationship in order to avoid a move toward more independence.

This decision to not leave analysis always begs the question of what may be avoided through such analytic arrangements. For example, is the patient wanting to retain a sense of a parent who is caring for them and loving them? Related to that set of wishes is a matter that I have seen in a number of patients for whom the sense of taking for granted the care of an analyst is deeply gratifying to the patient. In fact, it may overlap with what Winnicott referred to as the pleasure of wasting time or having time to waste. It may also involve holding on to grievance toward parents by creating a kind of reparation act, a permanent arrangement that compensates for what was not earlier given.

I worked with a male patient for 15 years, Ian, who was 21 years old when he began analysis. He had made great use of analysis over this period of time and had become significantly less depressed and more creative in that time. He had also found a relationship with a woman whom he loved and enjoyed being a father and a successful physician.

Ian stated that he never wanted to leave his analysis. In fact, he had declared frequently that he wanted me to never retire or die. He joked that even if I retired, we would continue our work, enjoying the logical inconsistency in his remark as well as the extraordinary specialness that it revealed. While over the years he had reluctantly cut down his hours from five to four to two times a week, he said repeatedly that this was as infrequent as he could bear seeing me.

In my countertransference, I had a difficult time determining what I was providing Ian at this point in his life, at least with regard to helping him understand himself. I was aware of my great affection for him and that we had withstood a great deal of turbulence in his transference experience during the first seven years of our relationship. I had gone from being experienced as rejecting and persecutory to someone whom he loved and felt loved by.

Ian's childhood had been mostly fraught with conflict about feeling coerced by his parents to believe whatever they said. His mother had rejected him quite strongly as he turned ten years old or so because he began expressing his independence in various ways. He had religious beliefs that, even by age ten, were questioning his Jewish Orthodox upbringing, and after his Bar Mitzvah, which he reluctantly completed, he wanted to be done with any form of religious activity. While his father was upset by Ian's direction, he remained loving and connected with him, except when they were both in the presence of Ian's mother.

Ian found his father's attempts to speak to his wife about not being so harsh toward Ian quite weak and ineffectual. Ian was quite estranged from his mother through the rest of his time spent living with his parents and in his adult life until her death several years into his analysis. His mother had remained quite close to Ian's older sister and brother, who had remained in the Orthodox community.

Ian's transference when we began was quite negative. He was silent for many sessions and felt that I was fake and unavailable. He didn't want to trust me even though he knew that he was trusting me to some extent by attending his analytic sessions. It was obvious to Ian that at least partially, he held a maternal transference to me. In this transference experience, he had some conviction that if he trusted me, he would be burned. Some of his attacks on me were humorous and imaginative, but some were difficult for me to bear. When he was being imaginative and funny, I had the sense that he was operating with more trust and awareness that parts of his experience were issuing from a sense of transference. Put another way, in these moments, I felt that he was better able to hold the paradox of incompatible realities from the past (his mistrust toward his mother) and present (his growing trust toward me in the here and now of analysis).

Obviously, in this moment of holding paradox, the temporal dimension of the transference has changed. For many years, Ian and I were only in his past experiences with his mother and family. There was no capacity to take me in as his analyst except through my provisions in the setting (e.g., Bleger, 1966; Cooper, 2019). When Ian had access to his own sense of humor, he was already holding a psychic reality in which he could safely make fun of me, I could bear it, and we could be together in a place of his love and hate.

My aim here is not to detail Ian's analysis prior to a particular moment that I want to take up. The particular matter that I want to take up is the moment when I felt as though it was difficult to ask questions about why Ian was remaining in analysis. It became clear to me over time, and I think clear to Ian, that as he was feeling much better about himself and me, he was trying to replicate a relationship with me that was like a family he had not really had.

It wasn't as though Ian was oblivious to the possibility that he was trying to negate or even obliterate painful experiences and his family through our continuing relationship and, as it were, his new family. I was reminded of a comment made by Jorge Luis Borges (1976): "The past is indestructible. Sooner or later all things come back and one of the things coming back is the project of abolishing the past" (p. 1).

I took up how much he wasn't only wanting to be able to experience something good about being known by a symbolic and actual parent in me but that he might wish to obliterate the past. While Ian agreed to some extent, it also seemed to me that Ian's sense of wasting his time and my time was, from his point of view, time well spent. He wanted to have a parent whom he could take for granted and waste time with. I was to abide by this arrangement and this gratification, regardless of its meaning. I told him that I thought he was seeking a kind of act of reparation that would be offered as his due. I suggested that he felt he deserved this reparation, but even more, that he was demanding it with me.

I find that these contexts with patients are extremely challenging. The analyst, in trying to promote the potential rewards that his patient might experience in terminating at some point, may be cast into the role of a rejecting, uncaring other. This is especially disturbing when in fact the analyst has usually worked quite hard to provide the patient with good analytic work.

I have an informal, anecdotal sense that many analysts continue to provide treatment for patients in these contexts. They feel it is just too difficult to actively take up these matters and that the analyst's fear of or concern with the patient's propensity to get angry or feel rejected dominates the analyst's thoughts about helping the patient to work through these conflicts.

I have been on both sides of this dilemma. At times, I have been able to actively take up the patient's resistance to further growth. Sometimes there is resistance in the patient's insistence to continue as a holding on of grievance or that justice is served by the memorialization of grievance through a permanent treatment. There are great opportunities during a termination process for patients to work through their deep sense of grievance about what has happened to them through analyzing the patient's resistance to termination. I have also been on the side of avoiding taking these matters up for long periods of time before either I or the patient became more able to take it up.

I also have a few patients for whom our quite lengthy analytic work feels essential to their continued growth. It is not time wasted.

In the case of Ian, I could speak to him about how understandable it was that he never wanted to leave. He also was aware that he didn't want to move into deeper levels of mourning what had happened to him. We talked about how he wanted to be Mother Time or Father Time in his analysis, and that now, in an even deeper way, after all we had been through, he couldn't trust me (and his mother again in the transference) to have him in mind. How could he trust whether I was suggesting termination in order to get rid of him versus trying to help him?

Ian did not take up these matters in a hurry. He enjoyed talking to me very much and to some extent luxuriated in the experience of having me, taking me for granted (and symbolically a loving parent), and being in control of our setting. I know that he could sense how much I enjoyed meeting with him and how important to me he had always been. I paid attention to whether this became annoying to me or taxing in some way.

Eventually, he set a termination date, catalyzed by ensuing college expenses for his daughter. He told me that he "reserved the right to come back," an interesting claim since it was always there for the taking in relation to his termination. In this sense, Ian continued to feel a sense of mastery over what had once been a dreadful experience of helplessness in relation to parental love.

My point in bringing up the matter of how patients engage in the use of time, or the illusion of unlimited time as gratification, is again to illustrate another dimension of the illusory use of time in analytic work. Ian even laid claim to future time in securing a promise that he could return, a promise that was already there for the taking. Here is an example of a patient who is finding something that had been obvious, unseen, and could now be taken in, in real time.

References

Akhtar, S. (1996) "Someday" and "if only" fantasies: Pathological optimism and inordinate nostalgia as related forms of idealization. *J Amer. Psychoanal. Assn.* 44: 723–753.

Bleger, J. (1966) *Symbiosis and Ambiguity*. London: New Library of Psychoanalysis, Routledge.

Bonowitz, C. (2021) What makes time fly: Loewald's concept of time and the resuscitation of vitality. In *Vitalization in Psychoanalysis: Perspectives on Being and Becoming,* ed. A. Cooney and R. Sopher. London: Routledge, pp. 72–91.

Borges, J. L. (1976) *Otras inquisicioones.* Madrid: Alinza Editorial.

Cooper, S. H. (2014) The analyst's capacity to bear disappointment with special attention to repetition. *J. Amer. Psychoanal. Assn.* 63: 1193–1207.

Cooper, S. H. (2018) Playing in the darkness: Use of the object and use of the subject. *J. Amer. Psychoanal. Assn.* 66(4): 743–765.

Cooper, S. H. (2019) A theory of the setting: The transformation of unrepresented experience and play. *Int. J. Psycho-Anal.* 100: 1439–1454.

Cooper, S. H. (2023a) *Playing and Becoming in Psychoanalysis.* London: Routledge

Cooper, S. H. (2023b) The play of mourning. *J. Amer. Psychoanal.* 71: 61–82.

Frosch, S. (2002) The other. *Amer. Imago.* 59: 389–407.

Grossmark, R. (2018) *The Unobtrusive Relational Analyst.* New York: Routledge.

King, P. (1973) The therapist-patient relationship. *Journal of Analytical Psychology.* 18: 1–8.

Kristeva, J. (1989) *Strangers to Ourselves.* London: Harvester Wheatsheaf.
Laplanche, J. (1997) The theory of seduction and the problem of the other. *Int. J. Psycho-anal.* 78: 653–666.
Laplanche, J. (1999) *Essays on Otherness.* London: Routledge.
Loewald, H. W. (1972) The experience of time. *Psychoanal. St. Child* 27: 401–410.
Ogden, T. (2024) Rethinking the concepts of the unconscious and analytic time. *Int. J. Psychoanal.* 105(3): 279–291.
Parsons, M. (1999) The logic of play. *Int. J. Psychoanal.* 80: 871–884.
Scarfone, D. (2015) *The Unpast.* New York: The Unconscious in Translation.
Slochower, J. (1996) Holding and the fate of the anlayst's subjectivity. *Psychoanal. Dial.* 6: 323–353.
Symington, N. (1983) The analyst's act of freedom as agent of therapeutic change. *Int. Rev. Psycho-Anal* 10: 283–291.
Winnicott, D. W. (1951) Transitional objects and transitional phenomena. In *Playing and Reality,* ed. D. W. Winnicott. New York: Basic Books, 1971, pp. 1–25.
Winnicott, D. W. (1958) The capacity to be alone. *Int. J. Psycho-Anal.* 39: 416–420.
Winnicott, D. W. (1968a) Interpretation in psychoanalysis. In *The Collected Works of D. W. Winnicott,* ed. L. Caldwell and H. T. Robinson. Oxford: Oxford University Press, pp. 253–258.
Winnicott, D. W. (1968b) Playing: Its theoretical status in the clinical situation. *Int. J. Psycho-Anal.* 49: 591–599.
Winnicott, D. W. (1969) The use of an object. *Int. J. Psycho-Anal.* 50: 711–716.
Winnicott, D. W. (1971) Playing, creativity and the search for the self. In *Playing and Reality,* ed. D. W. Winnicott. London: Tavistock, pp. 56–63.

7 The Virtual Oedipal Citadel

Varieties of Isolation, Oedipal Conflict, and Cover-Up

Over the years, I have worked with a number of patients who experience varieties of interpersonal avoidance. These forms of avoidance often masquerade as social anxiety about being with people, a complex overlay to Oedipal fixations and concerns. Unique elements of personal isolation are a relatively common clinical problem in working with neurotic patients, casting light on a kind of continuum of withdrawn states ranging from the patients I will explore here to more severe schizoid disturbances described well by Fairbairn (1952) and Guntrip (1969).

I aim to elaborate on fantasies and defenses which protect some patients in their Oedipal fixations and, in so doing, to explore a set of dynamic intersections between Oedipal conflict, withdrawn states, and interpersonal avoidance. These patients play in some relatively unique ways that I will try to explore. Some of these defenses, including elements of personal isolation, serve to conceal unconscious gratification of an Oedipal fantasy and relation. I'm especially interested in what distinctions we can make regarding varieties of aloneness in our consulting rooms. When Winnicott (1958) wrote about the capacity to be alone, he was referring to the capacity for the depressive position, a kind of psychological health and one in which the individual is able to feel impulses with equanimity and not too much repression in the presence of the other. In such states, the patient can tolerate the separateness of the other – in analysis, chiefly separateness from the analyst. In contrast, the patients I have in mind here experience elements of isolation, sometimes even cultivate it, in order to preserve a fantasy and, undoubtedly, some experiences of actually being loved.

The Oedipally fixated individual renounces others in favor of their unconsciously held romantic fantasy with a parent. In fact, the gratification that they experience in unconscious fantasy sometimes prevents them from finding new relationships that borrow from the regard that they have felt with a parent. Instead, they dwell inside a cocoon of self-sufficiency and love with the parent, renouncing real and new relationships with others. However, they are not psychically living alone in the ways that patients do with deeper self-loathing and deprivation, nor do they think that they deserve to live alone. Their actual exile or isolation permits the perpetuation of an unconscious fantasy of being with the object.

DOI: 10.4324/9781003569985-8

The patients I describe engage in forms of cover-up of Oedipal conflict. These forms of cover-up are so substantially protective because they serve not only to obscure an early exclusionary form of love but one that may also partly protect the desired object's frailty or vulnerability. Desire is also covered up to insulate oneself from an observing third party that might challenge the forbidden connection and its exclusive hold on the patient's erotic object choice. At the same time, avoidance of new experiences with objects not only protects both erotic and narcissistic gratifications in unconscious fantasy, hidden in plain view, but also serves to shore up the narcissistic vulnerability of the desired parent.

Thus, a coverup applies to both the intense love toward the Oedipal object, both known and unknown, as well as to the links between parts of the self within the subject's own unconscious (e.g., Freud, 1923). These parts are often equated with a destructive and forbidden, erotic connection that is linked to dangerous realizations. In this sense, the patient is wary of an observing thirdness that might overturn or disrupt the exclusionary fantasy of sole possession of the object and the object's hold on the patient's erotic object choice. What then makes this defensive organization so formidable are the myriad ways that the individual is protecting both erotic and narcissistic gratifications in unconscious fantasy that are experienced as essential to the subject.

Finally, there is another element to the unique forms of cover story I highlight here, a type of virtual patina whose refractory qualities arise from a certain conscious pride related to being held in the parent's regard, its forbidden connection, and its exclusive hold on the individual's object choice. Anxiety about the threats of an observing third (the analyst) or a third in the form of a new erotic object choice (or new experience with the current object choice) has been defensively converted to conscious pride in isolation. Analytic work may often help to bring the patient from defensive coverings of these kinds into a better position to appraise and mourn what has been lost.

I refer to this cluster of phenomena described in this paper as a virtual citadel, in part because these patients partly know that their experience and behavior are motivated by an unconscious fantasy. They are often in conflict about these fantasies, as they are also capable of sometimes being self-reflective about them. There is a mirage-like quality to these covers, at once a protective barrier that is also illusory. There is a kind of gray area between unconscious fantasies and a capacity to "know" about them – or to tip others in the direction of knowing them.

These forms of Oedipal conflict involve a subtype of a more general cover-up typical of Oedipus (e.g., Pilikian, 1974; Steiner, 1985). Pilikian (1974), a theater director in London who intrigued Steiner, stated in an interview "that everyone knows that Oedipus is not about the revelation of truth but about the cover up of truth. Everybody knows who Oedipus is from the start and everybody is covering up." Freud drew upon the Oedipal myth and the Sophocles play as akin to an analytic process in which the patient's unconscious gradually comes to be revealed for the patient. Steiner (1985), building on literary analysis by Vellacott (1971), argues that additionally at the heart of the Oedipus myth and Oedipal conflict is the notion that each of the participants, for their own reasons, turn a "blind eye" to the cover-up that was staged.

Steiner presents clinical material from a non-psychotic patient who, while able to view reality, is prone to misrepresent reality in order to elevate a fantasy of triumph over his father that allows him to be his mother's favorite. The patient does so, however, at the level of not facing interpersonal and professional consequences related to preserving this fantasy. Steiner borrows from Freud's (1940, p. 202) discussion of a psychical split, on one side between a view of reality and on the other an instinctually driven distortion of reality in which "the influence of the instincts detaches the ego from reality." In Freud's description, the two sides exist at the same time with each other.

Steiner (1985) helpfully views these instances as reflecting a failure to mourn the intrinsic loss in Oedipus, a loss that, in turn, prevents movement toward the depressive position. Steiner points out that the patient feels there is nothing to fear or lose because no crime is acknowledged to the self, only that a cover-up will be exposed. I have found the notion of cover-up that the literary critics Pilikian (1974), Vellacott (1971), and Steiner elaborated on to be quite relevant to most Oedipal conflict. I aim to delve more into some kinds of cover-ups that seem to require elements of the patient's renunciation of others or of parts of the self that are reinforced by elements of personal isolation.

One type of Oedipal fantasy features how these patients reject others, knowing and not knowing that it is because they consciously and unconsciously enjoy the love and regard of an Oedipal parent. They eschew actual relationships that they unconsciously fear would threaten the hold they feel on that parent. This hold is an illusion since the psychic forfeit involved in preserving these unconscious fantasies already suggests pain and disappointment regarding the unresolved nature of Oedipal conflict.

A variation on this theme involves how the individual protects the fragility of a desired parent. The neurotic sometimes unconsciously fears that the only way for them to preserve an unconscious alliance to a parent is to avoid contact with others. A new real relationship is feared as a threat or disruption to the unconsciously held relationship to the Oedipal parent, a relationship that the individual must uphold not only for their own gratification but also for the care of the desired other. Freud (1923) described how in having to give up a sexual object, the individual pursues an alteration of his ego, "which can only be described as a setting up of the object inside the ego" (p. 29).

Interestingly, a form of destructiveness of love is to some extent present in Oedipal conflict, refractory to analysis for very particular reasons. The displacement of love away from the original object onto another takes on the status of a new, forbidden object that cannot be realized in the reality of the patient's life. This withdrawal of love from the original object, while not frankly destructive, marks a step away from what contributed to the individual's well-being and, as is often the case, what is perceived by the individual as the well-being of an Oedipal parent. The fear of destructiveness of love then, the failure to reach the depressive position, renders it difficult to penetrate.

Since Klein's and Winnicott's massive contributions to psychoanalysis, it has been more common in our literature to discuss ways that "false," neurotic structures cover up much more profound and developmentally earlier varieties of disturbance. Winnicott's (1960) "True and False Self" paper and his largely neglected paper, "Interpretation in Psychoanalysis" (Winnicott, 1968) are so clinically useful because they alerted us to the idea that often much more serious disturbance can be covered by healthier elements of the patient's adaptation. Winnicott also emphasized that the analyst "can only talk to the False Self of the patient about the analyst's True Self." He provided a well-known example of a patient with whom he was able to discuss the patient's "non-existence" for the first time, an existence hidden away to others and to the patient.

Contextualizing these two Winnicott papers, it is important to understand that Winnicott was offering a more general critique at the time of psychoanalytic theory and practice as having valorized Oedipal conflict over developmentally earlier, usually more profound, versions of disturbance. He was concerned with the analyst's unwitting collaboration with the patient's "ego-defense" mechanisms rather than finding dimensions of a patient's sense of non-existence.

In my view, one of the distinct elements of play, which Winnicott saw as an overarching framework for conceptualizing analysis, is that it often involves a kind of spontaneous responsiveness of the analyst, one that is directed toward deeper elements of unconscious fantasy and defense that are themselves often bound inside transference-countertransference enactments with the analyst (Cooper, 2019, 2022, 2023). In this sense, then, play is what allowed Winnicott to reach deeper elements of the patient's psychic life than accessed through conventional interpretation.

Moreover, Winnicott was broadening the definition of defense itself (Cooper, 1989). He was trying to describe defenses not simply organized against id impulses which had been well explored by Freud (1894), Anna Freud (1963), and Klein (1975), among others. He was arguing that some defenses are erected against failing caretaking objects, objects who cannot be trusted by the child. Here, I additionally emphasize that the matter of "defenses organized against objects" is not unique to primitive pathology but is also true of Oedipal fixations. All defenses are organized to mitigate particular kinds of affects and impulses in the context of particular object relations. Specifically, some of the defenses I highlight here are also organized to unconsciously buoy up the fragilities of a desired parent even as they gratify exclusionary erotic fantasies.

I now examine a few brief clinical vignettes from the point of view of transference-countertransference engagement, highlighting forms of aloneness and isolation that are characteristic of some Oedipally oriented fantasies.

A Note on Oedipal Dynamics

It is worth noting that in my own experience, the objects and roles of objects in Oedipal dynamics are not always so clearly defined as Freud (1917) asserted. While one parent is often more identified as the object of desire and another parent a competitor, there are clearly desires being experienced toward each parent. In each of the examples that I provide, the parent who poses competitive challenges to the individual may also be the object of many desires and needs; these needs go beyond the familiar notion that the competitor parent should provide identificatory opportunities for the individual to help with the acceptance of loss accompanying Oedipal development.

For example, the parent with whom the individual competes is often also an object of affection and longing as well as an object of hostility and frustration. Along these lines, I have worked with many patients who feel simultaneously the wish for their mother's affection, but sometimes they are also competitive with their mothers for their father's affections. So, it is always important to keep in mind that the binaries between desire and competition, as well as between desire and hostility, are highly schematized versions of our relationships with our parents. Added to this complexity is the obvious fact that many of us desire women, men, or both. This is a subject in its own right that I cannot do justice to in this paper, though some of the clinical examples do illustrate the ways in which we hold multiple forms of longing and hostility toward our parents within Oedipal dynamics.

With regard to the varieties of aloneness that I am exploring here, most Oedipal fantasies of aloneness excite and preserve a feeling of elevation in the eyes of others or the other, such as the desired parent, or of superiority in relation to the Oedipal rival. Yet as analysis progresses, we often see that when the aloneness that the patient has experienced is becoming increasingly more uncomfortable (better for the evolving process of analysis), the patient feels more sadness about the distance that they experienced toward their Oedipal rival.

The neurotic's experience of aloneness is based less in self-loathing than in preserving his or her experience that they are loved or lovable; in fact, it can often be accompanied by feelings of grandiosity. These defensive efforts prevent grieving limitations within their complicated love relations (e.g., Steiner, 1985). At times they have also not been able to identify with the parent who has won the affections of the desired parent. Sometimes patients come to feel that the anger they experience toward a parent with whom they have felt competitive is related to sadness about wishing that they could have been better seen and helped by that parent. This process can better permit mourning and movement toward the depressive position.

Clinical Vignette

Anna

Anna began analysis at age 33 because she felt sad about pushing away her desire for available men. She married for the first time at age 37 and was quite content in her marriage at the time of this material.

Much of the first few years of analysis related to how much Anna spoke of preferring to go to social events alone. She would sometimes notice and enjoy that men found her attractive. She was excited by thinking about them wanting her but also felt rejecting of them for wanting her. Some of her masturbatory fantasies began with thinking about a man masturbating while thinking about her, a man whom she'd seen noticing her from an evening out. She was excited about being wanted by this man but could not feel how much she might want someone. As we understood some of these fantasies together, Anna could begin to feel more her own sense of wanting to be wanted from within a real relationship, not only a masturbatory fantasy.

Anna was often asking the question in analysis, "Why don't I really want to see my friends and have a romantic partner? I feel that maybe I should want someone more than I do, but I don't know whether I really do want someone."

Anna's father was a quiet man whose intelligence was understated. He adored Anna but was often absorbed, supporting his wife's needs to take up a great deal of interpersonal space in family interactions. Anna felt that her mother was always featured in stories and narratives of the family during her growing-up years. Her mother's career was much more public in scope than her father's work as a physician. Her younger brother and father were there as her mother's appendages. While Anna felt seen and understood by her father, she felt left outside her parents' relationship. Everything seemed fundamentally organized around them. She and her younger brother were told to go outside to play on weekend mornings, which Anna realized/fantasized as she grew older was likely in order to give her parents time to have sex. She remembered feeling sad to have to leave the house but never knew exactly why she was sad.

Anna always felt that she and her father had a special connection to each other. Anna was contemptuous and critical of her mother but hid it from her father. Instead, she lived inside a fantasy that her father really loved her more than her mother and, moreover, that she was the kind of woman he really wanted.

When Anna began analysis, she had accumulated a long list of unavailable men, including professors and a physician, whom she had held crushes toward for many years prior to analysis. When she dated men who were genuinely interested in her, she felt reflexively rejecting and often contemptuous of their needs. She could feel herself fantasize and sometimes feel desire toward men who were neither available to her nor actually that interesting to her in reality. The men she found most compelling to talk to and spend time with activated a desire in her to pull away. Anna did not express conscious desire toward me nor experience sexual fantasies, but she felt "comfortable" and "close" with me in ways that she had been able to feel with many unavailable men. I think that in some ways she held a compromise formation, familiar to her in other relationships with men, in which I was held at bay as both an object of desire who would threaten her relationship to her father as well as an observing third who might pose danger in relation to her conscious and unconscious fantasies.

A dream marked a transitional period when Anna began to feel more consciously lonely, wanting more closeness with a man, and at times alone in my presence. In the dream, she is feeling drawn to an older married man, but she is also uncertain whether or not she is attracted to him. A close female friend of hers is also in the dream, and she is ambiguously involved with this man. The man has bought Anna's friend a jacket of some kind. Anna is feeling guilty about possibly having sex with a married man, but she likes him and feels that the only way for her to find out about whether she is attracted to him is to have sex. She is anxious and troubled in the dream because she also doesn't know whether her friend is romantically or sexually involved with this man.

I remarked: "You've built in extra layers of protection from being with someone available." I said, "that it wasn't enough that he was married; that you would have to overcome your feelings about that; that your friend might be involved with him; and that you didn't even know whether you were attracted to him or not." She said with a combination of laughter and sadness, "You can never be too careful!"

As Anna began to experience more of her own loneliness, and the psychic forfeit of her adaptation, I felt an interesting type of aloneness in my countertransference reactions to her. I have felt it before when I experience a kind of defensive self-sufficiency that is beginning to wane and shift toward more relatedness both with me and in the patient's relationship to others. Interestingly, as I felt more of my aloneness with Anna, I began to notice how much I felt her remove from her own needs for closeness and sadness. I felt that I too was missing knowing her more deeply. Her dream underscored for me an actual feeling of trying to reach her inside her citadel, paradoxically, a more intimate experience of how she had held me at bay in the transference. The dream also seemed to mark an opening, what Green (1975) termed a ventilated space, that might allow us more opportunity to discuss and feel her isolation *together*.

In some other ways, the dream brought to the fore a way that I had missed understanding elements of Anna's communications about her isolation and sadness. Wilson (2006) has suggested that some of the ways that the analyst fails to see the patient is an evocation of lack. Further, if these experiences of lack can be experienced and explored by patient and analyst, there is a new opportunity for experiences of the depressive position and one's self as a unique person.

At the time of the dream, Anna was beginning to feel a sense of sadness about not seeing a particular man she had begun dating (a man who later became her husband). It started to feel silly to her to push him away as she had done with so many men because she knew that he was remarkably strong and independent as a person. I began to think that Anna was mourning her attachment to her father, the unavailable man whom she could only have in fantasy. She was starting to feel toward this new boyfriend that she would be losing something in reality, and the reality loss was weighing more heavily on her than preserving the unconscious fantasy of being with her father and unavailable men.

This transition marked a significant development in her analysis. My guess is that a good enough object in me as her analyst and her new male friend in the outside world allowed for the release of the "object inside the ego" (Freud, 1923, p. 29).

Now in analysis three years later, Anna was beginning to feel the same kind of sadness toward her friends for the first time. At the time of this vignette, Anna was becoming more sad about "wanting to want" but not wanting a close relationship with two friends who openly expressed their wish to see her more often. She felt that there was something missing inside her in terms of her desire to be with others whom she enjoyed being with. They wanted to spend more time than an hour-long walk with her. Sometimes, they wanted to hug her upon greeting and parting in a way that she could not easily warm up to.

Anna would observe how much they would miss her when they didn't see each other, email, or speak by phone. Anna was beginning to be more incredulous about her own remove and also in more conscious conflict about it. We began to understand together that when Anna had opened herself up to her husband, he then became part of her self-sufficiency, allowing her to be with him but still preserve elements of not needing others. They had each other, and she didn't want to need anyone else. She expressed some of this feeling in relation to me as well, feeling that between her husband and me, she wanted to feel content. This begged the question that I expressed about whether wanting to feel content with what she had was the same as actually feeling that she had enough.

Anna was realizing that she felt a more open contempt toward these women wanting to see her. I began to understand that her contempt included an identification with her mother's contempt for vulnerability, in contrast to some of the contempt that she had felt directed toward her mother. Anna had taken what she could take from her mother with regard to identifying with her, but it left her unable to connect with others as deeply as she wished and especially now toward her female friends. What was hidden in plain sight was Anna's projection onto these women of a childhood self that had wished for more maternal support. Her Oedipal love, albeit gratifying and nourishing, covered a larger story, a patina-like cocoon concealing her longings. Projection onto others of these longings allowed her to actively reject them as embodied in her isolation.

I refer to the covering here as virtual because it may also be seen as a play within a play of unconscious defense. Inside her use of disavowing or renouncing her own needs was an identification with her mother, hidden in plain sight. The virtual citadel is the result of feeling isolated and not able to experience more directly her most difficult feelings of desire, longings, and hostility with each parent. Anna began having more access to feeling her mother judging her when she was sad as a child. She recalled that her mother would say, "stop moping," when Anna felt a bit sad or lost about what to do with her time. Anna and I wondered if this was something that might have been said when Anna had felt banished from the home so that the parents could be alone. We better understood that Anna wished to not appear needy, leading her to keep a distance from her friends and their wishes to be close. Beyond that, though, this was an unconscious way to actually be close with her mother through identifying with her mother's judgments of others for being needy.

Anna could now more deeply sense that she was experiencing her friends as a needy part of herself. While this was something that Anna was likely intellectually aware of, she became more intimately aware of her mother's rejection of her sadness and longings. Her contempt toward her mother morphed into sadness, and the opportunity to acknowledge how she had not felt seen by her mother. As we explored these matters in depth, Anna began to see that she had good reason to not believe in the reality of the hugs that were offered by her friends as warmth and love. She was rejecting what she thought did not really exist.

In many ways, an early aloneness and sense of exclusion/banishment had been transformed into a valorized, prideful self-sufficiency, while her childhood self was abandoned. She had turned the sow's ear of her sadness into a pseudo-silk purse of self-sufficiency.

Anna's aloneness and the Oedipal virtual citadel did more than serve as a defensive structure providing gratification of her fantasy that she and her father were together. Her self-imposed exile from intimate relationships had also allowed her to keep distance from the pain of her mother's rejection. As she mitigated this pain relative to her mother, she had identified with her mother's contempt for those who needed too much. I imagine that if this contemptuous part of her mother had been less prominent, Anna would have felt more help in her struggles to accept her parents' relationship and their limitations in loving her (e.g., Britton, 1992). The citadel entailed distancing herself from her sadness and pain relative to her rivalry with her mother at least as much as it protected Anna's desires for her father.

Anna demonstrated elements of humility (loss of her defensive pride in her Oedipal choice) and reparation in the experience of relinquishment of her sense of specialness. In this progression, she was increasingly able to use me as a containing resource in her transit from Oedipal fixation to a greater acceptance of reality and limit.

Hannah

Hannah was a 24-year-old female graduate student, a highly intelligent and successful person who came into analysis feeling that she was often hiding her thoughts and achievements. In her close relationship with her boyfriend, she was uncomfortable being quicker to understand facts and ideas as well as often solving practical matters more quickly. In parallel fashion, she was also uncomfortable beating him in tennis and often resisted his wish to play actual games because she knew, and also knew that he knew, that she was a better player. This was apparently far more uncomfortable for her than him. When they played doubles with other couples, she did everything possible to set him up to actually claim the point when she could have easily resolved the point earlier. In singles, she also often tried to camouflage her abilities.

Similarly, in conversations with her boyfriend and others, Hannah would often be hypervigilant to not demonstrate a superior breadth of knowledge. One day early on in her analysis, as she described some relief in being able to speak openly with me about this and not hide as much, I said something like, "So are you trying to come clean here, wanting to be able to show your strengths and intelligence here without having to hide it?" She said without missing a beat, "What makes you think that I'm not doing to you what I do to my boyfriend." I said, "You mean setting up the point for me to have the illusion that you're doing something different or that you and I are doing something useful together." Hannah said, "Of course, you're playing with a pro here."

Hannah's analysis began in this way with what is likely familiar to you in the peek-a-boo and hide-and-seek of analysis and of defenses themselves. In our play, she is the expert at a game I am just learning. In this moment, she and I both know that she came to see me to be able to feel more comfortable with her intelligence and her aggression. We both know that her actual, full-throated competitiveness is already coming out in her one-upmanship regarding setting me up for the point. I am not going to ruin the play at this early point because we are hoping to find something together that might really make a difference.

I have come to appreciate how much these forms of play are part of the analysis itself, often more than finding out what she and I already know (Winnicott, 1968). As is true in *Oedipus Rex*, there is a story that she is covering up that is not so hidden to the participants but whose particular qualities I do not yet deeply understand. For example, in paying attention to and honoring Hannah's opening comment, is she inviting me into a transference to a father or boyfriend who needs to be protected? Is she asking for a particular protection from an observing third who might disrupt her eroticized Oedipal relationship?

We both already know that she adored her parents but felt that her mother was subtly disappointed in Hannah's father's achievements. We both also already know that Hannah shored up her father's self-esteem through her genuine love and admiration for him. So she has yet to grieve this element of her parents' relationship, her father's depression that is lodged inside her and that she feels colonized by when she engages in conversational and tennis banter with her partner and with her elderly male psychoanalyst.

This form of a manic defense seems to be yielding, as I am able to note with Hannah that she sometimes looks and sounds sad after we engage in our banter. Play brings us to the places where we used to laugh but now permits sadness and the potential for mourning. I will eventually be able to say to her in a meaningful way, "The pain you're staving off when you fail to claim knowledge or victory has already happened. Your boyfriend is much more able to bear his feelings that come with sometimes losing to you, but you didn't want your father to feel that way. You didn't have a way of even articulating this for yourself back then."

Play that Hannah has introduced and that I have tried to meet has allowed her to begin to mourn that her mother was disappointed in some ways with her father and her father with himself and Hannah's mother. She is trying to mourn that this is not a point that she can win, but at the same time, she doesn't have to avoid winning her own points. In my view, play involves transit toward mourning here. It is a game of peek-a-boo, hide-and-seek, nip-and-bite while feeling the inevitable sadness required in mourning this very thorny fault line in her parents' relationship (Cooper, 2023).

Hannah has partly created me as the old paternal object she had, someone who needs to be protected and shored up, but also a new object that she needs now – one that she wants to have stamina and to tolerate being destroyed. She institutes the familiar rules of her family involving her mother's open disappointment with her husband and Hannah's need to protect him. Even when she is admitting to this pattern and seeking help, she has to revert to "Gotcha" with me, and I am to survive losing the point or simply enjoy her making the point. The virtual citadel, however, seems to be moving from being an open secret to something that she feels as a familiar part of her adaptation.

As analysis developed further, Hannah was becoming a bit more open about her abilities with her boyfriend. One day I noticed that after an interpretation that I don't recall, Hannah said, "good point." We laughed regarding our history of discussing her approach to winning points. I think that we were both heartened that she had let go of some of her problematic covering up of her own abilities, which might have been why praising me for the point was funny. This comment, "good point," that on the face of it has an element of teasing, may have also expressed her recognition of me as a good object, one capable of providing some functions of reparation and protection that were compromised in her early life.

I was left, though, with a nagging feeling, one that I felt a bit curious about. Specifically, I was also annoyed that she had said "good point," and I realized for one of the first times that it was something she said with some frequency.

Without knowing exactly why, I wondered with her whether her mother said "good point" sometimes, and Hannah said with some excitement that her mother said it frequently. She talked about how evaluative her mother was of everyone, most of all Hannah's father but including Hannah to some extent. I realized that our helpful focus on Hannah's defensive retreat from success, in order to buoy up her father, was more complicated. She was also identified with her mother's hostility and tendency to be evaluative or even imperious. I was now experiencing a new set of countertransference experiences with Hannah that had not been apparent in our earlier discussion of how she hid her successes. We were entering into a kind of lack in our awareness (Wilson, 2006), an area of what had been covered up, though apparent, was not all that had been covered up. This led to a great deal more mourning, now including her identification with her mother which she had latched on to, in order to avoid being angrier with her than she already was. As Steiner (1985) highlighted, generally the patient's attempt to cover up challenging affects such as loss or feeling defeated is what prevents mourning and movement to the depressive position. Open acknowledgment of such loss is a prerequisite to the capacity to mourn.

Embedded in our earlier forms of play together was a level of Hannah's unconscious hostility and superiority that was obscured for me by her feeling that she had to hide her talents. When I inquired about her mother, I must have been feeling something about some elements of her identification with her mother that had been expressed and had served as resistance to further mourning. The work with Hannah exemplifies some of the ways in which play is inextricably linked to enactment, even as it sometimes illuminates elements of defense and unconscious fantasy (Parsons, 1999; Cooper, 2021).

I underscore that Hannah maintained a feeling of solitude in trying to preserve her attachment to her father. She was able to let me into her secret, a secret that kept her isolated to some extent from her boyfriend even as she disavowed her awareness that he likely already knew her secret. Through bits and pieces of a slow analytic process, Hannah became better able to acknowledge the paradox that she was keeping a secret regarding something that was not a secret to her father, her husband, and me. A virtual citadel was crumbling.

Jonathan

Jonathan, a 32-year-old man, was a handsome, intelligent, and athletically oriented person who felt growing up that he had to minimize or keep secret from his father many of his capacities other than his intellect. Jonathan's father had been a highly successful student but had few friends in high school and no girlfriends. Jonathan often felt that his father perked up around his son's intellectual interests but was disappointed in Jonathan's interest in social activities and his avid interest in sports. Jonathan felt a global dread about his father seeing these parts of him since he recognized his father's contempt toward many people who were more social and lighthearted than his father. Jonathan felt quite supported by his mother on many fronts, but she also tended to defer to her husband, which disappointed Jonathan. Jonathan and his mother shared a sense of humor and tended to do outdoor activities together, which provided him many pleasurable memories.

Jonathan was sought after by girls and boys during high school but always felt that he could engage only so far. By his last years of high school, Jonathan realized that he was more sexually attracted to males than females in his cohort. He noted with me early in his analysis that he had come out to his parents with little difficulty by the end of high school but that he had never "come out" in terms of how much he valued his social self in general. In young adulthood, Jonathan's renunciation of others in order to curry favor with his father hardened and was reinforced by his overwhelming success as an entrepreneur. He worked long hours and avoided close contact with most people except for a few casual sexual relationships.

As Jonathan's analysis developed, he came to understand that his father was envious of his son. However, Jonathan also knew that he had sought refuge from paternal criticism by, in some ways, feigning his lack of interest in group activities and socializing. Over the course of our work, Jonathan realized how much his mother had agreed to minimize her interests in social activities in deference to her husband. Jonathan also realized in a new way that he and his mother had kept hidden how much fun they had together. They laughed at each other's habits and their jokes and deeply enjoyed each other's minds. In some sort of unspoken conspiratorial alliance, this affection had been hidden, mitigated by their concern with Jonathan's father's reactions.

Jonathan and I began to note how much his renunciation of a social self had been linked to keeping his powerful love for his mother minimized. What passed in his family as his father's contempt for the "social" was now more deeply seen and experienced as his father's dislike for the passionate relationship between Jonathan and his mother. His seeking aloneness had reinforced his gratification with his mother and insulated his fantasy as well. We had been more focused on how much he had sought his father's love and approval.

In many ways, Jonathan made use of me as an object with whom he could be "social," by which we understood someone with whom he could be intimate, express desires, sadness, hostility, and curiosity. Over the course of our work, he moved from locating all wishes to be close as residing in me to feeling his own desire. He could criticize me for being in a "soft," "talky" kind of profession. In this mode, he pretended to not have such needs. He was "entrepreneurial and hard," and I was "soft and weak."

Jonathan's "cover-up" was again so interesting because it was an open secret that he held such needs and had always kept them in hiding. I had always been let in on the secret but was being asked to accept these projections and attributions as well as the disavowal of his own needs. Over the course of our work, analysis helped Jonathan to work with these forms of projective identification. He became able to get acquainted with the needs he contemptuously located in me as a part of him. He could see even more than he always had how much he had identified with his father's contempt and treated me as he had felt treated by his father. He could feel how much loss was involved in covering up the open secret that he enjoyed people, friendships, and intimacy linked to his loving relationship to his mother.

The work that Jonathan and I did together was also reinforced by the therapy that his mother engaged in concurrently with our work together. His mother and father eventually decided to separate and divorce during his analysis. Jonathan's mother had long felt that she was hiding too much of herself in order to preserve her relationship with Jonathan's father. Jonathan was inspired by his mother's courage and vulnerability, which helped him to soften his renunciation of his own emotional needs. Yet in the later phases of his analysis, he experienced anger toward his mother for the first time. While he had always been disappointed by his mother's deference to her husband, now he was experiencing how much it angered him that she didn't stand up for herself or him in relation to his father. He stopped blaming his father so entirely for what had occurred within his family and could better mourn his own regrets about submission, hiding, and isolating himself from others. He could also permit more feelings of disappointment toward his mother, whom he also loved a great deal.

I felt during this phase that I had not seen in the countertransference a kind of conscious and unconscious siding with Jonathan and his mother against the father. I was also a part of the cover-up, and this lack of awareness may have contributed to his delays in mourning his disappointment with his mother.

Jonathan's mother's renunciation had allowed him to partially use that as an excuse to avoid his own desires, greed, and anxieties about wanting more. Neither his father's contempt nor his mother's renunciation was the full story regarding why he had relied so much on personal isolation and putting his needs for intimacy and erotic life on hold.

As he attempted intimate relationships more frequently, he could take more responsibility for his own anxieties and fears of wanting too much. Jonathan was edging closer to the depressive position, one which entails coming to terms with lack and the risk of lack, as described by Wilson (2013).

Discussion

I have tried to highlight a particular quality that links each of these vignettes, namely a characteristic of patients with "cover" stories of aloneness or self-sufficiency. Anna knew that she was covering up by not wanting to desire or need another; Hannah was concealing her abilities despite these being apparent to those who knew her; and Jonathan covered up his "social" needs, which partly related to his barely concealed love affair with his mother.

While the notion of Oedipal conflict intrinsically involves a cover-up, a matter that Steiner (1985) so elegantly captured, by no means do all Oedipal cover-ups relate to personal isolation. The Oedipal virtual citadel that I have suggested here emphasizes cover-ups in which the other, and specifically the analyst in the analytic process, is asked (without explicitly asking) to not penetrate the patient's defensive self-sufficiency. These forms of self-sufficiency reflect isolation in the service of maintaining unconscious and conscious Oedipal fantasies. These examples point to elements of transference love that both incorporate the analyst into the role of a desired parent as well as an observing third, sometimes welcome and sometimes unwelcome. Not to be confused with the schizoid's citadel, which protects others from being destroyed by the toxic effects of their longings, the Oedipally fixated individual generally requires the citadel to preserve gratification within the isolating constraints of Oedipal fantasies.

Elements of my own countertransference experience helped to provide linkages to less accessible parts of each of these patients. For example, with each of the patients, I was struggling to find entry points with their defensive self-sufficiency. I was a witness to how they each simultaneously titrated needs and longings, protected Oedipal fantasies, and communicated "Do Not Enter" signs to the objects in the patient's life, including me.

Anna's self-sufficiency created feelings of frustration in me, and when she began to feel more of her own genuine isolation, I could feel sadness and a more vivid sense of her loneliness and in my experience of her. Hannah's form of play regarding the illusory hiding of her open secret created feelings in me of having to play along (until I didn't). Jonathan's form of projective identification engendered my wishes to suitably contain his projections until the point at which I could more actively help him to see that he was both ridding himself of scary desires and disavowing core parts of his identity.

Even more importantly, though, it is through the analytic process and the patient's experience of the analyst's capacities to hold the patient's various affects that the virtual citadel and its accompanying defensive structure start to yield to other experiences. For example, Hannah's banter with me was always in part related to the question of whether I was like her father, a man she believed required her to hide her own power and capabilities. However, when the banter turned to her comment, "good point," she was also recognizing me as a good object capable of providing her protection and some reparation that had been lacking earlier in her life.

Hannah may also have been experiencing me as "counter-dreaming" (Meltzer, 1973; Bergstein, 2013). In counter-dreaming, I was attempting to not be dulled by her repetitive banter so that I could sustain curiosity about the ways that she truncated our play. Both Meltzer and Bergstein describe the analyst's attempt to catch incipient meaning, often hearing words that we have heard before, such as "good point."

Each of these patients was able to develop trust in their analyst over time, marking a transition from trust in objects away from the egocentric investment in their isolation as a patina surrounding their Oedipal fantasies. Trust in the experience of good objects and creative investment in others is parallel to the movement toward the depressive position, one in which reality is no longer woefully inadequate when compared to the supreme, fantastic, Oedipal love that had been so firmly protected.

An important part of Sophocles' original play is related to the collusion of those surrounding Oedipus in covering up what was already known by all characters. While Jocasta consciously elevates belief in prophecies, she uses them in ways that are self-serving, rendering her blind in certain ways. Similarly, analysts need to keep an eye on many forms of enactment related to colluding in forms of cover-up. My own enjoyment of Hannah's banter may have been an obstacle to her being able to move more into depressive feelings of psychic forfeit and loss caused by her adaptation; it may have also facilitated her ability to progress and take this on. Since, by definition, we can't always know what is being enacted as it is occurring, what is most important is that the analyst tries to be curious about his or her countertransference to these cover-ups in order to find a way to be of use to the patient.

At a more general level, many analysts have elaborated quite incisively on the analyst's experience of the patient's Oedipal fantasies and defenses (e.g., Loewald, 1979; Britton, 1989; Bonasia, 2001; Davies, 2003; Gabbard, 2003; Cooper, 2003). Some of these authors have additionally explored, in kind, the Oedipal parent's experience of the child's Oedipal desires and hostility, as well as the parents' contribution to the child's Oedipal conflict. For example, in the cases of both Anna and Hannah, the passivity of the desired respective fathers is striking, and it is likely that the daughter's love and protectiveness toward their father contributed to the ways these patients developed sequestered experiences of isolation. In each patient, the father's perceived fragility catalyzed a sense of covering up just as much as their desires and love for their father. The parent with whom the child competes is often a more conspicuous focus for the development of conflict.

For each of the patients I have discussed here, the parent with whom the patient competes was a larger focus in earlier parts of analytic work. Over time, however, they each realized that the desired parent had contributed to elements of their personal isolation. Children need help holding both their desires and their competitive feelings in relation to each parent. The virtual citadel is often the result of feeling isolated and not seen in relation to their most difficult feelings of desire, competitiveness, and hostility with each parent in Oedipal triangles.

Each of the coverings that I have referred to here as a virtual citadel might be also seen as a play within the play of unconscious defense. I have tried to illustrate how I was brought into the play within the play in each vignette. It is interesting to note that the term "play within a play," or "meta-drama," derives from the French saying, "mise en abyme," or "placed into an abyss." Andre Gide referred to it as an embedded narrative. In some sense, all enactments, all embedded narratives, involve play within play, and here, it is only over time that the analyst discovers how they have participated in the cover-ups involving preservation of an Oedipal fantasy. Simultaneously, these cover-ups, in encountering the persistent demands of analytic work, help to reveal these cover-ups and find "ventilated spaces" (Green, 1975) in which to converse with elements of the patient's personal isolation.

When patients such as these come to work with us, we are privileged to be invited to enter their cover stories, even as they resist us doing so. They live inside their own privilege of having been loved, however imperfectly, by one and often both parents. In that way, they have never been alone in the ways that so many others have had to endure, especially those who have been deprived of the "land of the living" (Ogden, 1991).

References

Bergstein, A. (2013) Transcending the caesura: Reverie, dreaming and counter-dreaming. *Int. J. Psycho-Anal.* 94: 621–644.

Bonasia, E. (2001) The countertransference: Erotic, erotised, and perverse. *Int. J. Psycho-Anal.* 82: 249–262.

Britton, R. (1989) The missing link: Parental sexuality in the Oedipus complex. In *The Oedipus Complex Today: Clinical Implications,* ed. R. Britton, M. Feldman, and E. O'Shaughnessy. London: Karnac Books, pp. 43–58.

Britton, R. (1992) The Oedipus situation and the depressive position. *New Library Psychoanal.* 14: 34–45.

Cooper, S. H. (1989) Recent contributions to the study of defense mechanisms: A comparative view. *J. Amer. Psychoanal. Assn.* 37: 865–891.

Cooper, S. H. (2003) You say Oedipal, I say post-Oedipal: A consideration of desire and hostility in the analytic relationship. *Psychoanal. Dial.* 13: 41.

Cooper, S. H. (2019) A theory of the setting: Play and the transformation of unrepresented experience. *Int. J. Psycho-Anal.* 100: 1439–1454.

Cooper, S. (2021) Toward an ethic of play. *The Psychoanal. Quarterly* 90: 373–397.
Cooper, S. H. (2022) *Playing and Becoming in Psychoanalysis*. London: Routledge.
Cooper, S. H. (2023) The play of mourning. *J. Amer. Psychoanal. Assn.* 71: 61–82.
Davies, J. M. (2003) Falling in love with love: Oedipal and Postoedipal manifestations of idealization, mourning, and erotic masochism. *Psychoanal. Dial.* 13: 1–27.
Fairbairn, R. (1952) *Psychoanalytic Studies of the Personality*. London: Routledge.
Freud, A. (1963) *The Ego and The Mechanisms of Defense*. London: Routledge.
Freud, S. (1894) The neuropsychoses of defense. *SE* 3: 41–61.
Freud, S. (1917) The development of libido and the sexual organization. *SE* 16: 21–35.
Freud, S. (1923) *The ego and the Id*. *SE* 19: 13–68.
Gabbard, G. (2003) Playing with the reality of analytic love: Commentary on paper by Jody Messler Davies "Falling in love with love" July 2004. *Psychoanalytic Dialogues* 14: 503–515.
Green, A. (1975) The analyst, symbolization, and absence in the analytic setting (on changes in analytic practice and analytic experience) – in memory of D. W. Winnicott. *Int J. Psych-Anal.* 56: 9–22.
Guntrip, H. (1969) *Schizoid Phenomena, Object Relations, and the Self.* New York: International Universities Press.
Klein, M. (1975) *Envy and Gratitude*. New York: The Free Press.
Loewald, H. (1979) The waning of the Oedipus complex. *J. Amer. Psychoanal. Assn.* 27: 751–775.
Meltzer, D. (1973) The apprehension of beauty. *Cont. Psychoanal.* 9: 224–229.
Ogden, T. H. (1991) Some theoretical comments on personal isolation. *Int. J. Psychoanal. Dial.* 1: 377–390.
Parsons, M. (1999) The logic of play in psychoanalysis. *Int. J. Psycho-Anal.* 80(5): 871–884.
Pilikian, H. I. (1974) Interview with Douglas Keay, following production of Oedipus Rex. *Chichester Guardian Newspaper,* July 17.
Steiner, J. (1985) Turning a blind eye: The cover up for Oedipus. *Int. Rev. Psychoanal.* 12: 161–172.
Vellacott, P. (1971) *Sophocles and Oedipus: A Study of Oedipus Tyrannus*. London: Macmillan.
Wilson, M. (2006) Nothing could be further from the truth: The role of lack in the analytic process. *J Amer. Psychoanal. Assn.* 54: 397–421.
Wilson, M. (2013) Desire and responsibility: The ethics of countertransference experience. *Psychoanal Q.* 82: 435–76
Winnicott, D. W. (1958) The capacity to be alone. *Int. J. Psycho-Anal.* 39: 416–420.
Winnicott, D. W. (1960) ed. Ego distortion in terms of true self and false self. In *The Maturational Processes and the Facilitating Environment*. New York: International Universities Press, pp. 140–152.
Winnicott, D. W. (1968) Playing: Its theoretical status in the clinical situation. *Int. J. Psycho-Anal.* 49: 591–599.

8 "Being Careful in Only a Perverse Way"

The Use of Aesthetic Experience in Psychoanalytic Work

My title is taken from one of Richard Diebenkorn's (1995) list of ten notes regarding his artistic intentions in his "Notes to Myself upon Beginning a Painting." Richard Diebenkorn is my favorite twentieth-century oil painter. He is also my wife's favorite oil painter, and she is herself an oil painter and a psychoanalyst. So, I am familiar with the pleasures of thinking about creative experience at the intersection of psychoanalysis and painting. My aim in this talk is to help to stimulate your own thinking about this intersection or to help put into words how you already do this. I think that it is useful to deconstruct some elements of our aesthetic matrix as we listen and do analytic work.

It is not uncommon for Diebenkorn's paintings to come to mind when I am listening to patients. I do have a print of one of his paintings in my office but it is out of my own sight line. I think this is so because while I am listening to patients and myself, I am in different emotional places at the same time. For me, Diebenkorn portrays Winnicott's (1968a) startling notion that the purpose of interpretation is to hold paradox rather than resolve it. He is constantly joining while simultaneously separating – shapes, colors, and ideas. His work embodies that remarkable Heraclitus metaphorical question: Does the river divide two properties or join them?

I think of many of Diebenkorn's paintings as the visual representation of the depressive position. His abstract works embody interpenetrating shapes seeking a modicum of harmony, but not seeking it too much. He embraces the trouble, the strains of interpenetrating subjectivities, minds, parts of self, psychic countries, and the like. He also conveys the immense beauty of these complex elements of subjectivity. His paintings are most likely to come to mind for me as I am listening to patients who are moving in and out of the depressive position, getting close and darting away, or settling into it in a more full-throated way.

When I refer to the strains of interpenetrating subjectivities, of different abstract shapes and colors finding a way to live together in Diebenkorn's paintings, I am put in mind of so much about psychoanalysis. When we try to make use of "the diseases of the field" (Civitarese, 2008a, 2008b), try to find underlying continuity between alpha and beta elements of our patients' communications, within the interesting gaps between our patients' ways of using words and our own; the spaces between concrete and symbolized

DOI: 10.4324/9781003569985-9

expressions of affect; or the caesuras between knowing and not knowing, we are as analysts in the activity of making something of a painting ourselves. We are trying to find a temporary coherence without it being a forced coherence, a permanent understanding or, even worse perhaps, an answer or understanding. I have referred to some of these activities as the "activity of neutrality" (Cooper, 2022a).

So Richard Diebenkorn has in some sense always been at the intersection of my love of art and psychoanalysis. He conveys and represents for me the way I try to hold complex feelings toward all those I love deeply (family, friends, and patients) and what is unknown and mysterious about them, including myself.

I wish that I could paint. A small consolation is that Diebenkorn is so imprinted in my mind that sometimes I think of him as a close friend. While I am better at music and language than painting, I have had a similar relationship to Bob Dylan's poetry and music in my analytic work, one that I will also take up later in this paper in connection with a clinical vignette. For me, poetry and art often come up, unbidden, in efforts to restore the containing function, sometimes when it is not operating as I wish.

Being careful in a perverse way captures for me the ethical demands of free association by the patient, by the analyst, and by the painter. We try to open ourselves up to whatever is coming, but we don't do it without concern and awareness of the process. We give ourselves over to a process that is always changing, including our concerns about the process. Even the notion that trying to free associate is a recommendation is at least somewhat contradictory or at least paradoxical. Freedom can't be ordered by fiat or conferred by someone who is not in our mind. We are the guardians of what is in our mind. In analysis, while we give ourselves over to the analyst as a guardian of the process, we do not do so without strain and ambivalence. As Parsons (2006, 2007) put it so beautifully, psychoanalysis is inherently a contentious process.

Knowing and becoming are partnered for Diebenkorn in the ways in which he is operating with his heart but also with an accumulated body of technical skill. Technique and craft, art and knowledge, knowing and being are partnered here.

When Diebenkorn states that he aims to be careful in only a perverse way, I think that he is saying that he works hard to open himself to the unknown, to trust in his creative process. Being careful in a perverse way, is, I think, a way that he is the guardian of that artistic setting just as we are the guardians of the analytic setting (Cooper, 2019, under review).

Diebenkorn's aesthetic expressions emanate from an appreciation of what I call the aesthetic of pain as crucial to our adaptation. This aesthetic of pain was conveyed so beautifully in Kristeva's (1992) "Black Sun." In our clinical work, we appreciate how twisted our patients' adaptations are, how wasteful too, before we can help the patient to let go of them a bit. Each of us as patients is an artist of our affliction, and we as analysts are trained to appreciate this art. Kristeva (1992) stressed that in order to express pain, one cannot allow the style to be completely harmonious, but one has to make the sound grate, strain, and limp. As she put it, "Stylistic awkwardness is discourse of dulled pain" (p. 27).

The aesthetic experience of being a psychoanalyst and a painter is one of being in a moment when the observing eye and the emotional eye become one. The aesthetic matrix is one involving a generative cycle of creativity and vitalization.

There is an experience of the tension between safety and danger in painting and clinical work. Diebenkorn's chaos, created by the way that the paints are disorganized and interpenetrating, is a kind of controlled chaos. He instructs us regarding the safety in representation. Diebenkorn tells us about how he and his patient find their colors in a session, a feeling place. I think that I find a color place or a place where things come alive in other ways. Winnicott (1968c), in a paper on cultural experience, referred to this place more generally in the title of his extraordinary paper, "The Place Where We Live."

Painters take the viewer "part way on the journey toward a cohesive narrative of color and form. The viewer can take these partly processed elements and co-opt them into his own aesthetic experience." Here, I think that we are very much in Winnicott's notion of interpretation and responsiveness. Winnicott (1968a) interpreted "at the limits of his understanding." He wanted to use interpretation to show the patient the limits of his understanding so that the patient can make use of what he has to say or not in whatever way is their way. Winnicott is paradoxically using interpretation of the patient to demonstrate how he has made use of himself and offering to the patient the possibility that he or she might or might not make use of him. Interpretation is a subjective offering at the limits of understanding.

I am turning toward connecting painting and psychoanalysis not only because it joins two loves but also because it highlights a certain reality, namely that we have many limitations in understanding psychoanalysis by writing strictly about psychoanalysis. One doesn't get at the unconscious so well through words or theories. In a recent and soon-to-be-published paper by Ogden (in press), he discusses the problems that occasion ever thinking of the unconscious as someplace other than what is being expressed now. He cites the poet Eluard (Ernst and Eluard, 1943) in saying "that there is another world, but it is in this one."

Our words have their place, but the story is incomplete. We are all using the idioms that are most meaningful to us – poetry, painting, sculpture, music, politics, and other idioms – to get at the ineffable.

A Personal Use of Poetry, Painting, and Fly Fishing in Clinical Work

I will try to get at some things about how I think outside psychoanalysis that come *into play* in my analytic work. Indeed, play is for me the most meaningful way to describe psychoanalytic process in general, both as the underlying logic of analysis and also in particular moments of intersubjective engagement. So I will try to get at some ways that I make use of and play with elements of associations to meaningful artistic work during clinical process.

For many years, I have been thinking about the relationship of Richard Diebenkorn's work, abstract expressionism in general, the poetry of Bob Dylan, fly fishing, and geographical locations that come to mind during analytic process to psychoanalytic work. I will say a word about each as they enter a consideration of aesthetics and my analytic work. I mention them here not because these artistic associations mark a single, aesthetic cluster, or in Palmer's terms, the aesthetic matrix that helps me with my work. It's just one axis among other types of reverie.

I am not always sure that the exercise of deconstruction is helpful to the patient or to me. I do know, however, that it is often quite enjoyable, and that pleasure feels like an intrinsic part of doing analytic work. I would even say that it is a part of being with my patients or coming to life with them from my side of things. This is a complex matter though, because I have sometimes wondered if my associations are a form of distancing, a disease of the field, as it were. It is always worth considering that possibility. Palmer has shown us an extraordinary version of his own aesthetic matrix that inspires me here to join him in my own way, to struggle to think about these matters.

I begin with the remainder of Diebenkorn's notes to himself because I will touch on a few as I reflect on my work. Part of why they are so compelling to me is that I think you will see that they are remarkably resonant with Winnicottian and Bionian intention in analytic work, a revolution in psychoanalytic thinking that I especially link with Donald Winnicott. Winnicott's courage to emphasize the actuality of the object (mother and analyst) marked a level of intellectual integrity that was astounding given the intellectual culture in which he lived.

While Winnicott and Bion are quite different in the way they work and their theoretical constructs, far beyond what I can explore in this paper, they shared a mistrust of words and formulation. Interestingly, while they were each interested in helping patients to better come to life or feel alive, they were profoundly different in their listening positions as analyst/artists. I will only say that Winnicott's (1968b) objections to Bion's (1967; 1970) instruction for the analyst to listen without memory and desire were based on the idea that Bion's words were taken from their reference to an Eliot poem, "The Waste Land," which references botanical objects rather than human beings.

Winnicott was more interested in the actuality of his experience and objects, and this grounded him in his orientation toward play. As Aguayo (2018) has highlighted, Bion's reverie and dreaming the patient increasingly came to integrate the mother and analyst as an actual object in addition to being projective entities.

Here are Diebenkorn's "Notes to Myself upon Beginning a Painting."

1. Attempt what is not certain. Certainty may or may not come later. It may then be a valuable delusion.
2. The pretty, initial position which falls short of completeness is not to be valued – except as a stimulus for further moves.
3. Do search. But in order to find other than what is searched for.
4. Use and respond to the initial fresh qualities but consider them absolutely expendable.
5. Don't "discover" a subject – of any kind.
6. Somehow don't be bored – but if you must, use it in action. Use its destructive potential.
7. Mistakes can't be erased, but they move you from your present position.
8. Keep thinking about Pollyanna.
9. Tolerate chaos.
10. Be careful, but only in a perverse way.

Regarding the first three of these notes, but especially the first, when I do have something to say, I do not generally know what I am going to say when I begin talking. I am "attempting what is not certain." I feel a modicum of comfort in speaking at these moments and sometimes even compelled to do so even though I don't know yet what I'm going to say.

What is happening now that I feel like I have something to say? The feeling is one of subtle activation that I can only vaguely liken to other experiences. In contrast to this kind of activation, I feel very activated when I become aware of feeling desirous of food or sex, wanting to go somewhere or to write something. I may also feel activated as in wanting to tear something down or, in a sense, start to build something. I am excited, and I feel filled with something even if I am not sure of what it is I am filled with. This kind of activation is usually milder, but I know that there is a desire that I've not quite yet found words for.

The thing that really stands out is trust. There is so much trust to begin to speak before knowing what I have to say. It has always been like this in my work, even though much earlier in my career, I would try to formulate so much more than I do now in advance of speaking. Even then though, when I decided to speak, there was a sense of trust in a feeling of there being something to say. I always enjoyed something attributed to Henry Kissinger when, as Secretary of State, he was asked about his views on a recent story about China. He stated, "I don't know what I think about it because I have not yet spoken on the matter." Many other analysts from various traditions have spoken to this feeling (e.g., Bromberg, 1996; Ferro, 2012).

Sometimes the experience of not knowing what I'm going to say lasts longer than others. There are times when, within a brief amount of time after feeling catalyzed or activated to speak, I have purchase on what I want to say.

Usually, these short latency times relate to something that is relatively better formulated because it overlaps with something that I've thought before. I'm hearing some similar themes or feelings that I feel an impulse to speak of. Not uncommonly, these are the kinds of things that I reflect on within myself to hold back from saying (e.g., Diebenkorn: "The pretty, initial position which falls short of completeness is not to be valued – except as a stimulus for further moves. Or do search but in order to find other than what is searched for"). It's good to know that painters, not only psychoanalysts, are aware that often what is most accessible is mostly banal. I'm very familiar with this fact of life in writing as well.

These experiences of feeling like I have something to say and the thoughts arriving quickly are perhaps more like what Winnicott (1968a) and other Independents such as Pearl King (1978) emphasized as the value in "waiting." Too often, I am going to say something that the patient already knows or that involves me wanting to demonstrate that I know something.

The instances of not knowing what I am going to say that involve not knowing for a longer amount of time are more anxiety-arousing. I really don't know what I'm going to say, but I feel that I have something to say. These experiences feel more likely to generate something original and creative in the interaction with my patient.

In contrast to these moments of not knowing, I have many familiar passages of poetry and visualized experiences that come to mind quite repeatedly. Even though these are familiar associations, they will often feel fresh because I don't yet know what they might suggest or why they came to mind. I think that they feel fresh because they are helping me to know where I am in a new experience with a patient. They feel to me often like as close as I can get with my patient to locating what Winnicott (1968c) might have meant when he described "the place where we live."

Clinical Vignette

Ms. A

Ms. A, 40 years old, was exploring herself in relation to her work, marriage, and mothering. She had been able to do a great deal of productive analytic work with me in the previous three years of analysis but continued to feel an anger about her parents' deceit and hypocrisy in her family. It had been difficult for her to release her parents and herself from adjudicating the wrongs that she felt they committed.

The youngest of four children, and four years younger than her next oldest sibling, Ms. A felt that she was exposed to her parents' deceit more than her three older sisters. When she was a sophomore in high school, she discovered that her mother had been having an affair with a married man from a couple who were close friends of her parents. At around the same time, she learned that her father had had several affairs with men and women. After learning of these affairs, she told her sisters, and while they were affected by the news, they were also much more preoccupied with their lives in college, graduate school, and romantic pursuits of their own. One of her sisters said that she had already been aware of their parents' extramarital relationships and "didn't care."

Ms. A had what she regarded as a strong marriage, but she sometimes compared her own marriage to what she imagined was mine. The leading edge, though, of her interest in mine had some notable qualities. I never felt that she was particularly curious about my wife or our relationship except in relation to her painful feelings regarding her own sense of her parents as a couple. She established my marriage as a positive, loving union, but with seemingly no flesh or color. It seemed to me that she referred to my marriage as a kind of frozen entity, benignly "good," but not really a living, breathing relationship between two people. She also never seemed to express explicit wishes to be my romantic partner, nor did she compare herself to my wife. In other words, she seemed less interested in breaking into my coupledom than in wishing that her parents had been in a relationship more similar to what she fantasized about mine.

At times, I would internally think about this quality of frozenness and be a bit puzzled as I listened to Ms. A. I never felt that she had a strong erotic transference nor palpable curiosity about me or my wife. Instead, over time, it seemed to me as though she might be trying to establish the possibility of a solid parental couple, and that her concerns or interest in my marriage had in it a sense of exclusion or pain related to the deception of being left out of secrets. When I reflected on some of these thoughts with her over the years, she seemed interested, but there was little elaboration.

At the time of this vignette, Ms. A had been curious about how I spent free time in New York. She was wondering if I was going to theater and basketball games, which were each of particular interest to her. As I listened, I thought how she seemed to want to know what I was seeing or not seeing.

Then she asked if I still rooted for the team that she rooted for, asking this question because I had recently moved to a new city. I listened as I thought that she had now shifted from a curiosity about what I was seeing to how loyal I was. Did I move on easily, or did I remain loyal?

Then she became more animated and returned to the question of whether I had seen a particular play. Her speech was more pressured than usual. I might have easily continued to listen or wondered aloud with her if she was also curious about with whom I did whatever activities I did, but I did not. In retrospect, her tone in questioning me about this felt a bit pressuring, and I had a sense that she wanted to know what I was doing. At one point during a session, she was wondering again what I had been doing, fantasizing about whether I had seen a particular play that she was interested in. Without thinking and apparent "activation," I somewhat clumsily said, "We saw that play." Ms. A was disturbed that I had used the pronoun "we," and I was quite uncertain why as well.

Over a series of sessions, Ms. A became angry with me about being thoughtless and careless about the likely reference to my wife. I sometimes answer questions that my patients have about whether I've seen a film or play or read a book, though it is not as consistent as likely some analysts are about whether they answer directly, or immediately look into why a patient is asking what they are asking, or both. Regardless of whether I answer a question such as this, I try to remain curious about the patient's response and my motives in answering or not answering a question such as this. I was certain, though, that it was unusual for me to use the pronoun "we."

This event marked a period of lively associative material from both Ms. A and internally from me as I tried to listen and consider what had happened between Ms. A and myself. Ms. A was angry and agitated about my thoughtlessness, but she was never very specific about what bothered her about the use of the word "we." I felt a surprising initial sense of internal impatience with Ms. A's reactions, especially noteworthy because I felt concerned that I had needlessly caused Ms. A disturbance through my reference to my coupledom with my wife.

I became curious about what I was feeling. As I considered what Ms. A had been communicating with her question about what I had seen in my free time, I had the sense that Ms. A had engaged in an unconscious protean effort to revisit her parents' relationship in a deeper way. I thought about the words in her questions of "what had I seen," and I began associating more to what she had seen and not seen (I will say more about this shortly).

Ms. A began speaking of how she had previously enjoyed thinking about activities that I would engage in with my wife. She hadn't realized that she thought often about my going to the theater or sporting events with my wife and that this was quite satisfying for her to fantasize about. She said that something made her feel very anxious and overwhelmed when I actually acknowledged the reality of my wife when I used the word "we." Ms. A said, "it makes me want to tear you both down."

If Ms. A was moving into efforts to revisit her parents' relationship, she didn't realize that she was doing this and was consciously expressing again that she was victimized by my acknowledgment of a reality that she already knew but didn't want to know – that I was married and might have things that she was deprived of in her parents' union. She had been unconsciously fantasizing about a new parental couple which had been threatened when it became too real.

Put another way, was Ms. A repeating something with me about knowing and not knowing what her parents were doing? Now she was doing so with her analyst, whom she knew was wanting her to be able "to see" as much of her inner experience as possible. My impatience seemed to ignore this protean curiosity and her attempt to help us explore her feelings.

What was most striking as this period developed was not Ms. A's anger but more my sense that she was more curious about her reactions to the word "we" than she had ever been before. It seemed as though something was opening up regarding Ms. A's anger, even though on the surface, she felt in the familiar position of grievance toward her parents' marriage and now mine. She knew that her wish to "tear down" my relationship was at odds with her previous fantasies of my union with my wife.

I was also interested in my own mind with the word "tear," which seemed to reflect her angry wish to deny her "tears." The word itself and usage seemed to contain the wish to deny sadness in the service of maintaining anger and grievance.

Ms. A had formed a good marriage herself and seemed to deeply love and feel loved by her husband. In some way, I think that she was remaining in a compromise in which her anger and grudge toward her parents would be forever institutionalized as a part of her grievance as psychic adaptation. Or was this my fear, that in the transference I was frozen as an older man whom she both knew and didn't know was in a couple? I think that this may have unwittingly motivated my use of the pronoun "we," which could be alternately seen as carelessness on my part or an unconscious introduction of reality that Ms. A and I were eliding. Here was the parental couple that she didn't have being put right in front of her. In retrospect, I could imagine that it would have been far more sensitive for me to be able to link her curiosity about what I was doing with the parental couple she was always longing for. I also wished that I could have listened for where she would have taken this.

During the period of these sessions, I found myself continually replaying a Bob Dylan (1965) song from 1965 in my mind, "It's Alright, Ma (I'm Only Bleeding)." Since age 14 or so, I have been a close reader/listener of Dylan, especially the imagistic poetry from 1964 to 1968. I've also read extensively in literary criticism related to his work. He has been a close companion since my latency age years.

There could be many reasons why this song/poem was coming to mind, but I was now linking my rekindled interest in the song at the time with Ms. A with the phase of work that we were in. It has come to mind a few times during analytic work over the years when I am beginning to experience my patients in something more akin to the depressive position or heading more that way than in our prior work. It is also common for me to have a number of Diebenkorn paintings come to mind in association with a patient's movement toward the depressive position, but the

Diebenkorn images are quite distinct from this poem by Dylan in how they come up. Unlike Diebenkorn's most complex paintings, this Dylan poem gets at a highly unstable attempt at mourning and grieving and holding paradox. Dylan is overwhelmed with what he is seeing, which is what is causing the instability. Diebenkorn's work reflects a much more stable, often more harmonious holding of the depressive position than the Dylan poem I will elaborate here.

In my opinion, "It's Alright, Ma (I'm Only Bleeding) (Dylan, 1965) is perhaps Dylan's strongest poem, from a period of his imagistic poetry from 1964 to 1968. In the song, his explicit audience is a mother for the ages, a mother who is witnessing his own attempts to view and ultimately integrate reality. He is staring into one of the grimmest views imaginable of politics, religion, hypocrisy, race relations, and gender relations in the United States in 1964. As he details all of these forms of lying, war, political and religious hypocrisy, and our suffering in the face of these egregious human tendencies, he ends each verse with a statement to his mother, "It's alright Ma, I'm only ..." and the words keep changing – bleeding, crying, moaning, sighing, and finally in the last stanza, "it's alright, Ma, it's life, and life only."

The mother/container has quite a task ahead. She is asked to hold his suffering, including that his mind is stuffed with images of his "eyes colliding with stuffed graveyards," murderous thoughts, and being "bent out of shape by society's pliers." At one level, his continued refrain of "it's alright, Ma" could be seen as a sarcastic lament about the inability of anyone to contain all this pain. Things are decidedly not alright. I see it more as an indication of the strains regarding his inability to accept reality. The movement of the poem is from "I'm only bleeding" to "it's life, and life only."

The structure of the song is one in which he elaborates that we require illusion to constitute some sense of forbearance and civilization. In each stanza, though, as illusion is detailed or erected, eventually it is torn down. Each stanza concludes with a note of forbearance, one directed to his mother, reassuring her that he will survive.

Dylan stages his need to tell his mother about all of the horrible things that he has noticed and is now cataloging. It's important to tell her about how bad things are and are becoming. His attempt to separate from her has left him alone, vulnerable, and he clearly wants her to know about this state of affairs. I think that a more complete view of the poem is one in which he is simultaneously expressing his wishes that she could have done something to make the world more wholesome and welcoming while fending off these wishes in order to more fully integrate that he is on his own.

He understands the bedrock principles of the reality principle even as he hates the dissemblance that people engage in in response to them.

There was a great deal here for me regarding Ms. A and our transference-countertransference engagement, specifically about the way that Dylan is simultaneously putting something in his mother's face (in all our faces) and yet, at the same time, lurching toward acceptance and equanimity without resignation. Ms. A had been repeatedly holding on to her grievance and putting it front and center in our work. Now, I was putting something in Ms. A's face, and the poem was helping me realize how much I'd been facilitating Ms. A's compromises. She had been holding on to her grievance and perhaps putting her grievance in front of the two of us and unconsciously her parents. Despite her substantial progress in her outside life and in her outside relationships, she was stultified in moving toward mourning the loss of a loving parental couple better able to help her. Ms. A had grown despite her sense that she could not trust authority, and it was this bastion of grievance that I think we were working on together when she asked her question.

Ms. A was communicating both the wish to know what I was doing when I'm not with her and the wish to not know what I was doing. My impatience with Ms. A's reaction was likely related to my wish for her to grieve what she didn't have. At this point in her analysis, I was not yet clear about whether she was angry that I might be lying about a good parental front or just trying to push away her awareness that I might have something that her parents didn't have. As time went on, it became much clearer how very painful it was for her to think about people who had parents who loved each other. She didn't want to have to mourn what she didn't have.

As I mentioned earlier, it is striking to contrast the Dylan poem and its emergence in the work with Ms. A, and the way that I sometimes associate to Diebenkorn's work when I am feeling a patient moving toward the depressive position. Diebenkorn's work feels as though it sits comfortably, albeit with some elements of melancholy, in the depressive position. Dylan's song is raging, aching, and bemoaning the fact that being a human is all just a lot to deal with. I think that the poem was a marker of what Ms. A was trying to do and not yet able to do. I was clumsily trying to find myself in Ms. A's efforts to work through more about what she didn't have. In this clinical moment, I was expecting her to be able to give up her grievance too quickly. Initially, I was not making my own enactment, as well as her anger toward me, matters of curiosity and potentially rich territory.

My guess is that the song came along when it did as a kind of soothing, holding experience for my own limitations in containment. It became an auxiliary container in mourning my own good and painful experiences with the parental couple. The words and music also brought me closer to Ms. A's considerable pain.

Discussion

I suppose in some ways, I have always been leaning into other modalities, such as art, music, poetry, and my passion for fly fishing, to find my patients. I rely on these immersive experiences because sometimes they pop up in ways that lay bare who a patient has become with me or that involve my becoming something other than who I was before. These other modalities are often essential in finding a level of unconscious communication that is occurring between patient and analyst.

Going on to a river is often a kind of religious experience for me. Heraclitus was correct when he said that no man ever steps in the same river twice. I wish that I could say that I approach every clinical hour that way, because I don't, but it is an aspiration to do so. Our work is an artistic process that we are creating together with our patients. Care is required, but freedom of thought is too; freedom to be subversive in thought; to honor and welcome the unexpected; and to tolerate chaos.

In fly fishing, the emergence of an insect hatch can signal that trout will begin to rise out of the water to feed. In the course of clinical work, sometimes the emergence of insect hatches comes to mind, usually at times when a patient is either beginning to open up a new area or emerging from stuck patterns and moving into something new. I will sometimes associate to days when nothing I am able to do on a river yields success when I am feeling stuck with patients. I often associate to the scenery on a river when I am feeling a level of relaxation with a patient. We are in a stream (of associations) together.

None of these links that I am making are so clear and distinct. Sometimes there is the possibility that I am simply associating to poetry, art, or fly fishing so that I might be someplace else than in the challenging clinical circumstance I am in. This is one way I make use of Diebenkorn's note to himself to be careful in a perverse way. We need to be careful to engage in self-reflection about our associations, but it is also, nearly always, important to get lost too. The use of art and poetry as part of our reverie may be its own version of a disease of the field or a caesura of sorts (Civitarese, 2008a, 2008b). For example, my puzzling internal anger toward Ms. A's anger after I used a pronoun that was hurtful to her was the beginning of a new process. In that process, I began linking her psychological efforts to look into her envy toward others who had loving parents as well as her resistance to doing so through the Dylan poem. But any of these imaginative referent points can be used defensively by the analyst as well, taking us in new and potentially generative directions.

And then, of course, there are times with patients in which there is the utter impoverishment of imagery from any of these wonderful avenues (e.g., Cooper, 2018). For patients who struggle with symbolization, it is especially difficult for me to find representation, metaphor, images, beauty, hideousness, and connection to other media in general. In fact, it is often in the mind of the analyst that symbolization starts to take form (Civitarese, 2008a, 2008b; Cooper, 2018, 2019), especially for patients who struggle with symbolization. Patience is required.

So many of Deibenkorn's (1995) insights about his aspirational position as a painter were those previously outlined by Winnicott and Bion regarding analytic work. Bion's admonition to make boredom itself a subject of interest mirrors Diebenkorn's comment about boredom being potentially generative. Winnicott's observation that he interprets to show his patient the limits of his understanding and Bion's (1962) suspicion of overly organized formulations (overvalued ideas and selected facts) remind me how much Diebenkorn resists things falling too easily into place.

I think that we all work with what we have regarding our imaginative potential. I have been unconsciously putting almost an obsession with Diebenkorn and Dylan to good use in my work, as is true for my interest in insects and fly fishing. A related matter is whether we also use psychoanalytic theories as a form of play in helping us to make sense of what we are learning from our patients (Cooper, 2015; 2017). This means that we also have to ask questions about whether the theory we hold may also involve a caesura of sorts.

In other words, theories themselves become part of an imaginative scaffolding for trying to listen to our patients in new registers. This view differs from a more usual view of theory as more exclusively helping us organize our experience. I think that seasoned and talented analysts have been able to internalize the ways that theory organizes so that it becomes a launching point for finding our own, creative ways of engaging with our patients. Theoretical faddism, which has always been a feature of practicing psychoanalysts, usually reflects the collapse of our analytic imaginations in the service of false knowing. We long for knowing, even when sometimes the theory we are desperately holding on to eschews not knowing!

In analyzing a patient, we are devoted to helping a person become the person they are, and are becoming. One cannot know in advance where any of that will go. Being careful but only in a perverse way seems about right. We must carry out extreme care to preserve an analytic setting in which that process of becoming and learning can evolve. We are guardians of that experience, but we must also be careful to not control the process and evaluate its requisite qualities of neutrality in too microscopic a way.

Helping another human being to grow is not an art project, but if we can't help someone to find the art and music inside them, then it is hard to feel that we have helped someone come to life in new and imaginative ways. For any of us to help a person come alive in new ways, we must awaken ourselves as much as possible to our own inner life that is emerging with our patient. Otherwise, it might be too much like being careful, but not in a perverse way.

References

Aguayo, J. (2018) D. W. Winnicott, Melanie Klein, and W. R. Bion: The controversy over the nature of the external object-holding and container/contained (1941–1967). *Psychoanal. Q.* 87: 767–807.

Bion, W. R. (1962) *Learning from Experience.* London: Tavistock.

Bion, W. R. (1967) Notes on memory and desire. *Psychoanal Forum* 2: 272–280.

Bion, W. R. (1970) *Attention and Interpretation.* London: Tavistock.

Bromberg, P. M. (1996) *Standing in the Spaces: Essays on Clinical Process, Trauma and Dissociation.* Hillsdale, NJ: The Analytic Press.

Civitarese, G. (2008a) "Caesura" as Bion's discourse on method. *Int. J. Psychoanal.* 89: 1123–1143.

Civitarese, G. (2008b) *The Intimate Room: Theory and Technique of the Analytic Field.* London: Routledge.

Cooper, S. H. (2015) Clinical theory at the border(s): Emergent types of theory in a post-pluralistic psychoanalysis. *Int. J. Psychoanal.* 96: 273–229.

Cooper, S. H. (2017) The analyst's use of theory: The play of theory in psychoanalytic theory integration. *J. Amer. Psychoanal. Assn.* 65: 659–582.

Cooper, S. H. (2018). Playing in the darkness: Use of the object and use of the subject. *J. Amer. Psychoanal. Assn.* 66(4): 743–765.

Cooper, S. H. (2019) A theory of the setting: The transformation of unrepresented experience and play. *Int. J. Psycho-Anal.* 100: 1439–1454.

Cooper, S. H. (2022a) The activity of neutrality. *The Psychoanal. Q.* 91: 355–369.

Cooper, S. H. (2022b) The limits of intimacy and the intimacy of limit: Play and its relation to the bad object. *J. Amer. Psychoanal. Assoc.* 70: 241–261.

Diebenkorn, R. (1995) Notes to myself on beginning a painting. Trudy Montgomery Gallery.

Dylan, B. (1965) It's all right Ma (I'm only bleeding). In *Bringing It All Home.* New York: Columbia Records.

Ernst, M. and Eluard, P. (1943) *Misfortunes of the Immortals.* New York: The Black Sun Press.

Ferro, A. (2012) Creativity in the consulting room: Factors of fertility and infertility. *Psychoanal Inq* 32: 257–274.

King, P. (1978) Affective response of the analyst to the patient's communications. *Int. J. Psychoanal.* 59: 329–334.

Kristeva, J. (1992) *Black Sun.* New York: Columbia University Press.

Palmer, J. (2024) The aesthetic matrix: A conversation between a painter and a Psychoanalyst. *Psychoanal. Inq.* 41: 327–337.

Parsons, M. (2006) The analyst's countertransference to the analytic process. *Int. J. Psychoanal.* 87: 1183–1198.

Parsons, M. (2007) Raiding the inarticulate: The internal analytic setting and listening beyond countertransference. *Int. J. Psycho-Anal.* 88(6): 1441–1456.

Winnicott, D. W. (1968a) Interpretation in psychoanalysis. Originally published in *Psychoanalytic Explorations*, ed. C. Winnicott, R. Shepherd, and M. Davis. Cambridge, MA: Harvard University Press, 1989, pp. 207–212; Also in, *The Collected Works of D. W. Winnicott*, ed. L. Caldwell and H. T. Robinson. Oxford: Oxford Academic, pp. 253–257.

Winnicott, D. W. (1968b) Letter to W. Bion. In *The Collected Works of D. W. Winnicott*, ed. L. Caldwell and H. T. Robinson. Oxford: Oxford Academic Press, pp. 157–158.

Winnicott, D. W. (1968c) The place where we live. In *The Collected Works of D. W. Winnicott*, ed. L. Caldwell and H. T. Robinson. Oxford: Oxford Academic Press, pp. 221–227.

Index

For Product Safety Concerns and Information please contact our EU
representative GPSR@taylorandfrancis.com
Taylor & Francis Verlag GmbH, Kaufingerstraße 24, 80331 München, Germany

www.ingramcontent.com/pod-product-compliance
Lightning Source LLC
Chambersburg PA
CBHW070349270326
41926CB00017B/4050
* 9 7 8 1 0 3 2 9 4 1 9 4 3 *